CW01551167

NINJA AIR FRYER COOKBOOK UK

The XXL Air Fryer Recipe Book with Quick, Delicious & Mouthwatering Dishes for Daily Enjoyment I incl. Vegan & Vegetarian I Nutritional Information I Favourites Collection

OLIVIA EDWARDS

© 2024 Olivia Edwards

All rights reserved

All rights for this book here presented belong exclusively to the author.

Usage or reproduction of the text is forbidden and requires a clear consent of the author in case of expectations.

ISBN – 9798339096016

TABLE OF CONTENTS

CHAPTER 3: MAIN COURSES

CHAPTER 4: SIDE DISHES

EXCLUSIVE BONUS

40 Weight Loss Recipes

&

14 Days Meal Plan

Scan the QR-Code and receive
the FREE download:

INTRODUCTION

Cooking at home doesn't have to be complicated or time-consuming, and the Ninja Air Fryer is here to prove it. Whether you're whipping up a quick breakfast before a busy day or preparing a full dinner for your family, this cookbook will show you how to turn simple ingredients into mouth watering meals—all with the magic of air frying.

The recipes in this book are designed for everyone, from novice cooks to seasoned pros. You'll find a delicious array of dishes that are easy to follow, nutritious, and, most importantly, packed with flavour. We're talking crispy golden potatoes, juicy chicken that's tender on the inside with the perfect crust on the outside, and even guilt-free desserts that taste like indulgences but are way lighter on the calories.

But this isn't just about recipes—it's about making cooking more fun and efficient. With the Ninja Air Fryer, you get to enjoy all the perks of fried food without the mess of deep-frying or the extra oil. And it's not just for frying! From roasting to baking to reheating leftovers, this appliance does it all.

Why the Ninja Air Fryer Rocks Your Kitchen

Let's get into what makes the Ninja Air Fryer such a powerhouse in the kitchen. Spoiler alert: it's not just for chips. Here's why this gadget is going to become your new best friend for breakfast, lunch, dinner, and everything in between.

1. Save Time and Make Cooking a Breeze

We've all been there—standing in front of the oven, waiting for it to preheat, then checking every five minutes to see if the food is done. With the Ninja Air Fryer, say goodbye to long preheating times and constant monitoring. It speeds up the entire cooking process without sacrificing flavour or texture. You can get meals on the table in half the time it takes with a traditional oven.

Let's face it—life's busy. Whether you're juggling work, kids, or just trying to keep up with the never-ending to-do list, dinner often feels like a race against the clock. The Ninja Air Fryer changes that. Its rapid air circulation means food cooks evenly and quickly, so you can spend less time in the kitchen and more time actually enjoying your meal. Even better, fewer dishes to clean!

2. Healthier Fried Food? Yes, please!

Love the crispy crunch of fried food, but not the side of guilt that comes with it? The Ninja Air Fryer gives you all the crunch and flavour you crave without drowning your food in oil. With just a little spray of oil—or sometimes none at all—you can enjoy fried favourites like fries, chicken, and onion rings with up to 75% less fat. Think of it as giving your comfort food a healthy makeover.

The air fryer doesn't just stop at fries, though. It's perfect for making lighter versions of so many dishes—crispy tofu, roasted vegetables, even crunchy falafel. You can enjoy all your favourite fried foods without the heavy feeling that comes afterward. And let's be honest, who doesn't love a good guilt-free treat?

3. The Swiss Army Knife of Kitchen Gadgets

The Ninja Air Fryer is not just a one-trick pony. Sure, it fries things to crispy perfection, but it's also a mini oven, grill, and dehydrator all rolled into one. That means you can roast a chicken, bake cookies, grill veggies, or even make your own dried fruit snacks. Whether you're a foodie who loves experimenting in the kitchen or someone who just needs to reheat last night's dinner, the air fryer has you covered.

It's the ultimate kitchen sidekick for meal prepping, too. You can batch-cook chicken, veggies, or grains and store them for easy meals throughout the week. The air fryer takes the guesswork out of cooking, so you can spend less time worrying about whether dinner will be a success and more time enjoying it.

4. Smaller Carbon Footprint, Bigger Results

Did you know the Ninja Air Fryer uses less energy than your oven? Shorter cook times mean less electricity or gas, and that's good news for both your wallet and the planet. Plus, by cooking more efficiently, you're also helping reduce food waste. No more dried-out chicken or burned veggies—just perfectly cooked meals every time.

It's not just about saving time and energy; it's about making your kitchen more eco-friendly. With less oil used and fewer pans to wash, you're cutting down on waste in more ways than one. And trust me, once you realise how easy it is to cook and clean with the air fryer, you'll wonder how you ever managed without it.

From crispy fries to perfectly roasted veggies, the Ninja Air Fryer is here to simplify your cooking and make it a whole lot more fun. In the next section, we'll explore the different models of Ninja Air Fryers, so you can get the most out of your machine, no matter which one you own.

Types of Ninja Air Fryers

Ninja has an air fryer for every kitchen and every type of cook, from small households to large families. Whether you're juggling multiple dishes at once or need a simple, no-fuss solution for dinner, there's a model designed to make your life easier. In this section, we'll break down three of Ninja's top air fryer models: the Double Stack Air Fryer, the 2-Basket Air Fryer, and the 1-Basket Air Fryer. Each one comes with its own strengths (and a few trade-offs), so let's find the one that's just right for you.

1. Double Stack Air Fryer: The Space-Saving Powerhouse

If you love efficiency and want to maximise your kitchen counter space without compromising on cooking capacity, the Double Stack Air Fryer is a total game-changer. With its innovative DoubleStack™ Air Frying technology, you can cook up to four foods at once in one machine, making multitasking in the kitchen a breeze.

Benefits:

❖ **Cook more, save space**: The Double Stack Air Fryer is like having two air fryers in one. It features two 4-quart baskets stacked on top of each other, giving you the power to cook different foods simultaneously without taking up extra counter space. In fact, this model is thinner than a typical air fryer, making it ideal for small kitchens where space is at a premium.

❖ **Ideal for variety:** Need to cook veggies and proteins at the same time? No problem. Load your vegetables onto the crisper plate, then insert the stacked rack and cook your proteins on top. Everything cooks evenly with that irresistible crispy finish, and there's no flavour crossover. It's designed for maximum versatility, so you can whip up multiple dishes in one go.

- ❖ **Family-sized meals:** Despite its space-saving design, this air fryer has plenty of capacity. You can cook 2 lbs of wings in each basket—enough to feed a crowd—making it a great option for dinner parties, family meals, or meal prep for the week.

Drawbacks:

- ❖ **More layers, more cleanup:** While the double-stack design is perfect for cooking multiple foods, it does mean more components to clean. You'll have to wash both baskets, the crisper plate, and the stacked rack, which can add a bit of extra time to the post-cooking routine.

2. 2-Basket Air Fryer: The Multitasker's Dream

Meet the 2-Basket Air Fryer—a powerful and flexible solution for anyone who wants to cook two foods, two ways, at the same time. Whether you're prepping dinner for the family or entertaining guests, the dual-basket design and large capacity make it easy to tackle big meals without breaking a sweat.

Benefits:

- ❖ **Smart cooking made simple:** With DualZone™ Technology, you can use two independent air fryer baskets to cook two completely different foods with separate temperatures and times. The best part? The Smart Finish™ feature ensures that both dishes finish cooking at the same time, so you don't have to worry about juggling multiple settings or dishes.

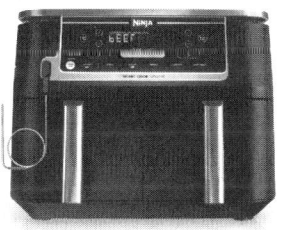

- ❖ IQ Boost for faster cooking: This air fryer doesn't just cook; it thinks ahead. The IQ Boost™ technology optimally distributes power between both baskets, allowing you to cook up to 8 lbs of chicken wings or a 6-lb whole chicken alongside a side dish in record time. Whether you're cooking for a big group or just want dinner done fast, IQ Boost has your back.

- ❖ 6 versatile cooking programs: The 2-Basket Air Fryer is more than just an air fryer. With six different cooking functions—Air Fry, Air Broil, Roast, Bake, Reheat, and

Dehydrate—it's a full-fledged kitchen companion. From crispy chicken to perfectly roasted vegetables to homemade dried fruit, you can do it all.

Drawbacks:

❖ **Limited for** oversized items: While the dual-basket design is great for cooking two foods at once, the size of each basket means you might have to cook in batches if you're preparing larger items like a whole roast. But for standard meals or family-sized portions, it works beautifully.

❖ Might take some monitoring: If you're cooking two different items that require adjustments (like flipping), you'll need to check on both baskets throughout the process. Not a big deal, but worth noting if you prefer a set-it-and-forget-it style of cooking.

3. 1-Basket Air Fryer: The Classic, Space-Saving Workhorse

The Ninja Air Fryer Pro XL is the perfect blend of simplicity and power. Don't let its single-basket design fool you—this air fryer still delivers incredible results with its MaxCrisp™ technology and 6.5-quart capacity. It's perfect for anyone who needs a reliable, easy-to-use air fryer for daily meals.

Benefits:

❖ **MaxCrisp** Technology for ultra-crispy results: Love that golden, crispy crunch? The Ninja Air Fryer Pro XL uses superheated air at up to 450°F to ensure your food comes out perfectly crispy, whether you're cooking frozen fries, fresh veggies, or even a batch of wings. With little to no oil required, it's an ideal choice for healthier meals that don't skimp on texture.

❖ 6-in-1 functionality: This air fryer does it all. With six cooking functions—MaxCrisp, Air Fry, Air Roast, Bake, Reheat, and Dehydrate—you can use it for everything from roasting vegetables to baking cookies to dehydrating fruit. It's compact, but don't underestimate its versatility.

Drawbacks:

- **Not ideal for multitasking:** With only one basket, you can't cook multiple dishes at once. If you like preparing your protein and sides simultaneously, you might find yourself cooking in batches or waiting for one part of the meal to finish before starting the next.

- **Limited capacity for large families:** While the 1-Basket Air Fryer is great for couples or small families, it might feel a bit limited if you regularly cook large meals. That said, it's perfect for quick weeknight dinners or smaller households that don't need to cook huge quantities at once.

Ninja Air Fryer Settings Guide

One of the standout features of the Ninja Air Fryer is its versatility. While many air fryers are designed to simply crisp up your food, the Ninja Air Fryer takes things to a whole new level with multiple settings that allow you to roast, bake, broil, dehydrate, and more. But with all these options, it can be a little overwhelming to know which setting to use and when. Don't worry, though—we've got you covered.

In this section, we'll break down each setting, explain how it works, and give you examples of when to use it. Whether you're frying up crispy snacks, roasting a full meal, or even dehydrating fruit for healthy snacks, this guide will help you master your Ninja Air Fryer.

1. Air Fry: The Classic Crispy Setting

The Air Fry setting is what made air fryers famous. Using superheated air, this setting mimics the effects of frying but with a fraction of the oil. The result? Perfectly crispy food without the guilt.

- **Best for:** Fries, chicken wings, mozzarella sticks, onion rings, and anything you want to be crispy on the outside and tender on the inside.

- **How it works:** The Air Fry setting rapidly circulates hot air around your food, creating a crispy exterior while cooking the inside evenly. With most foods, you'll need little to no oil—just a light spray is enough to get that golden crunch.

- **Pro Tip:** Flip or shake your food halfway through cooking to ensure even crispiness. You can also preheat the air fryer for a couple of minutes to get an even faster, more consistent result.

Example:

Cooking up some crispy fries? Preheat the air fryer for a few minutes, toss your fries with a teaspoon of oil (optional), and set it to Air Fry for 15-20 minutes at 200°C (390°F). Give the basket a good shake halfway through cooking for that perfect golden finish.

2. Air Broil: For that Perfect Char

The Air Broil setting is perfect for giving your food that charred, caramelised finish you'd typically get from a grill. If you love your food with a bit of colour and crispness on top, Air Broil is your go-to setting.

- **Best for:** Steaks, chicken breasts, vegetables like asparagus or bell peppers, and seafood like salmon or shrimp.

- **How it works:** Air Broil uses high heat to brown and crisp the surface of your food. It's like broiling in your oven, but with much faster and more even results. This setting is especially useful for finishing dishes that need a bit of a char without overcooking.

- **Pro Tip:** If you're using Air Broil for proteins like steak or fish, keep an eye on the cooking time. It works fast, so a few minutes on each side is often all you need for a perfectly seared dish.

Example:

Want a juicy, medium-rare steak with a nice sear? Season your steak, place it in the air fryer basket, and set it to Air Broil at 200°C (390°F) for about 8-10 minutes, flipping halfway through. Let it rest for a few minutes after cooking, and you've got yourself a restaurant-quality steak at home.

3. Roast: The Ultimate for Tender Meats and Veggies

The Roast setting is ideal for larger cuts of meat and hearty vegetables. It's perfect for slow cooking and tenderising food, with results that rival traditional oven-roasted dishes.

- **Best for:** Roasting a whole chicken, lamb chops, pork tenderloin, or vegetables like sweet potatoes, carrots, and Brussels sprouts.

- **How it works:** Roast uses lower, consistent heat to gently cook your food while maintaining its moisture. This setting is perfect for tougher cuts of meat or when you want to cook larger portions without drying them out.

- **Pro Tip:** For best results, use a meat thermometer to check doneness, especially for larger cuts of meat. You can also pair this setting with the Air Broil feature for a crisp finish.

Example:

Roasting a whole chicken? Rub the chicken with olive oil, herbs, and spices, and place it in the air fryer basket. Set it to Roast at 180°C (350°F) for about 60 minutes, flipping halfway through. For an extra-crispy skin, switch to Air Broil for the last 5 minutes.

4. Bake: Your Mini Convection Oven

The Bake setting transforms your Ninja Air Fryer into a mini convection oven, perfect for making cakes, muffins, cookies, and even casseroles. It's ideal when you don't want to fire up your full-sized oven but still crave freshly baked treats.

- **Best for:** Cakes, muffins, cookies, brownies, and savoury bakes like quiches or lasagnas.
- **How it works:** Bake uses steady heat from all sides to evenly cook your food, much like a traditional oven. However, the smaller size of the air fryer means it heats up faster and bakes more evenly, with less risk of burning.
- **Pro Tip:** Use air fryer-safe baking pans or silicone moulds for best results. Since the air fryer is smaller than a traditional oven, it bakes faster, so keep an eye on your goodies and adjust the time accordingly.

Example:

Craving some gooey chocolate chip cookies? Scoop your cookie dough into an air fryer-safe tray, set it to Bake at 175°C (350°F), and bake for about 8-10 minutes. The result? Perfectly soft and chewy cookies with crispy edges.

5. Reheat: Bring Leftovers Back to Life

The Reheat setting is a game-changer for leftovers. Unlike a microwave, which often leaves food soggy, the Reheat setting uses air circulation to restore the crispiness and texture of your food, making it taste like it was freshly cooked.

- **Best for:** Pizza, fried chicken, roasted vegetables, pasta bakes, or any leftovers you want to crisp up without drying out.
- **How it works:** The Reheat setting uses low, even heat to gently warm your food while restoring its texture. No more soggy pizza crusts or dried-out meats—just perfectly reheated meals.

- **Pro Tip:** For crispy leftovers, like fries or fried chicken, use the Air Fry setting for the last couple of minutes to restore that golden crunch.

Example:

Got leftover pizza? Set your air fryer to Reheat at 160°C (320°F) and reheat the slices for about 3-4 minutes. Your pizza will come out with a crispy crust and melted cheese, just like when it was first made.

6. Dehydrate: Healthy Snacks Made Easy

The Dehydrate setting is perfect for anyone who loves making their own healthy snacks. From dried fruit to beef jerky, this setting allows you to slowly remove moisture from food without cooking it, preserving its flavour and texture.

- **Best for:** Fruit slices, beef jerky, kale chips, and homemade snacks.
- **How it works:** Dehydrate uses low heat over a long period to remove moisture from food, creating a chewy, preserved texture. This is great for making dried fruit, jerky, or vegetable chips.
- **Pro Tip:** Slice your fruit or meat thinly and evenly for the best dehydration results. Arrange them in a single layer in the air fryer, and make sure to check on them periodically to prevent over-drying.

  Example:

  Want to make homemade dried apple chips? Thinly slice your apples, sprinkle with cinnamon, and set the air fryer to Dehydrate at 60°C (140°F) for about 6-8 hours. The result? Chewy, flavour-packed apple chips perfect for snacking.

Cooking Tips for the Ninja Air Fryer

While the Ninja Air Fryer has plenty of settings to make cooking easier, understanding how to use it like a pro can take your meals to the next level. Whether you're adapting a favourite oven recipe, experimenting with new dishes, or just trying to cut down on cooking time, these tips will help you get the best possible results from your Ninja Air Fryer.

1. Converting Traditional Oven Recipes to Air Fryer Instructions

If you've ever found yourself wondering, "Can I make this in the air fryer?" the answer is probably yes! Almost any recipe that works in the oven can be adapted for the Ninja Air Fryer, but you'll need to make a few adjustments to cooking times and temperatures. Here's a handy guide to get you started.

- **Tip 1: Lower the Temperature**

  When converting a recipe from the oven to the air fryer, you'll generally want to reduce the temperature by 10-20%. For example, if an oven recipe calls for cooking at 200°C (400°F), set your air fryer to around 180°C (360°F). The Ninja Air Fryer's compact size and powerful heat circulation mean food cooks more quickly, so lowering the temperature ensures it cooks evenly without burning.

- **Tip 2: Reduce Cooking Time**

  Air Fryers work faster than traditional ovens, so you'll need to cut down the cooking time. As a general rule, start by reducing the cooking time by about 25%. For instance, if a recipe says to bake something for 40 minutes, check it after 30 minutes in the air fryer. Keep an eye on your dish, and adjust as needed.

- **Tip 3: Preheat for Best Results**

  While preheating isn't always necessary, it can help ensure even cooking, especially for foods that need to be crispy on the outside and tender on the inside. Preheat your Ninja Air Fryer for about 3-5 minutes before adding your ingredients. This is particularly useful for dishes like French fries, chicken wings, or anything that benefits from a crispy exterior.

- **Tip 4: Don't Overcrowd the Basket**

  Just like in an oven, air circulation is key to perfect results. If you overcrowd the basket, the hot air won't be able to circulate properly, and your food may end up unevenly cooked or soggy. For best results, arrange your food in a single layer and avoid stacking whenever possible. If you need to cook large quantities, it's worth doing it in batches.

Example: Adapting a Lasagna Recipe

If you're converting an oven-baked lasagna recipe, you'd lower the oven temperature from 200°C (400°F) to 180°C (360°F), reduce the baking time from 60 minutes to about 45 minutes, and check for doneness halfway through. Using the Bake setting on the Ninja Air Fryer ensures the lasagna cooks evenly, with a perfectly golden top.

2. Maximising Crispiness: Tips for the Perfect Crunch

The Ninja Air Fryer is famous for its ability to create crispy, golden food with little to no oil. But if you want that restaurant-level crunch, there are a few tricks to keep in mind.

- **Tip 1: Use a Light Coat of Oil**

  While the air fryer works with no oil, using a light spray of oil on certain foods (like fries or chicken) can really elevate the crisp factor. A quick spritz with an oil spray bottle is usually all it takes. For an extra layer of crunch, you can also use oil with a higher smoke point, like avocado oil or canola oil.

- **Tip 2: Shake or Flip Your Food**

  To ensure even crisping, give your food a shake or a flip about halfway through cooking. This helps the hot air hit all sides and ensures the entire surface gets that beautiful golden colour. If you're cooking something like fries, wings, or roasted veggies, shaking the basket is essential for a perfectly crisp result.

- **Tip 3: Dry Your Ingredients Before Cooking**

  For foods like potatoes or chicken, pat them dry before cooking to remove excess moisture. This simple step helps achieve better browning and crispiness. Moisture is the enemy of crisp, so make sure your ingredients are as dry as possible before you start cooking.

3. How to Get the Most Out of Your Ninja Air Fryer Settings

We've already discussed the different Ninja Air Fryer settings, but here's how to make the most of them for everyday cooking.

- **Tip 1: Pair Settings for Advanced Cooking**

  One of the great features of the Ninja Air Fryer is its ability to combine settings for more complex recipes. For example, you can use the Roast setting to cook a chicken until juicy, then switch to Air Broil for the last few minutes to crisp up the skin. This gives you the best of both worlds—tender and juicy inside, with a perfectly crisp outside.

- **Tip 2: Experiment with the Dehydrate Setting**

  The Dehydrate setting isn't just for making dried fruit or jerky (though it's fantastic for that). You can also use it to crisp up herbs, create crunchy vegetable chips, or even make your own croutons from stale bread. It's a great way to get creative with leftover ingredients and make healthy snacks at home.

- **Tip 3: Reheat Leftovers Like a Pro**

  The Reheat function is perfect for giving your leftovers new life, but here's a trick: if you're reheating something that was originally crispy (like pizza or fried chicken), use the Air Fry setting for the last couple of minutes. This ensures you get that freshly cooked crispiness back, instead of the sogginess that microwaves usually leave behind.

4. Quick Meal Prep Hacks with the Ninja Air Fryer

Your Ninja Air Fryer is a lifesaver when it comes to meal prep. Whether you're batch-cooking for the week or just looking to streamline your routine, here are some tips to make it even easier.

- **Tip 1: Batch-Cook Proteins**

  Cook a large batch of chicken breasts, thighs, or even tofu at the beginning of the week, and store them in the fridge for quick meals. With the Ninja Air Fryer's Roast or Air Fry settings, you can cook up to 8 chicken breasts or several servings of tofu at once, making meal prep faster and easier. Then, simply reheat them with the Reheat function when you're ready to eat.

- **Tip 2: Make Big Batches of Veggies**

  Roasting vegetables in the air fryer is quick and easy, and the results are perfectly crispy and caramelised. Batch-cook a variety of veggies—like sweet potatoes, carrots, or Brussels sprouts—and store them in airtight containers. You'll have ready-to-go sides that just need a quick reheat before serving.

- **Tip 3: Freeze and Air-Fry**

  Did you know you can air-fry straight from frozen? Pre-cook items like chicken tenders, meatballs, or even French fries and freeze them. When you're ready to eat, just toss them in the air fryer, and they'll come out crispy and hot in minutes.

5. Cleaning and Maintenance: Keeping Your Ninja Air Fryer in Top Shape

Finally, let's not forget about cleaning and maintenance. A well-cared-for air fryer will last longer and perform better, so it's worth taking the time to keep it clean.

- **Tip 1: Clean After Every Use**

  It's tempting to skip cleaning after a quick meal, but regular maintenance will keep your air fryer in great shape. After every use, let the air fryer cool down, then clean the basket, crisper plate, and any racks with warm, soapy water. These parts are usually dishwasher-safe, so that's an easy option, too.

- **Tip 2: Don't Forget the Interior**

  Every so often, take a damp cloth and wipe down the interior of the air fryer. This helps prevent any build-up of grease or food particles that could affect performance.

- **Tip 3: Avoid Abrasive Scrubbers**

  When cleaning the non-stick parts of your Ninja Air Fryer, avoid using abrasive scrubbers or harsh chemicals. A soft sponge and mild soap are all you need to keep your air fryer clean without damaging its non-stick coating.

Storage and Reheating Tips

Whether you're cooking for the week ahead or dealing with leftovers, the Ninja Air Fryer can help you store and reheat food without sacrificing flavour or texture. While microwaves often leave food soggy or overcooked, the air fryer is a master at bringing dishes back to life. In this section, we'll look at some practical tips for storing your food and reheating it to perfection using the Ninja Air Fryer.

1. Storing Leftovers: Keep Food Fresh for Longer

Storing leftovers properly is key to maintaining flavour and freshness. Follow these tips to make sure your meals are as tasty when you reheat them as they were the first time around.

- **Tip 1: Use Airtight Containers**

  The best way to keep your leftovers fresh is to store them in airtight containers. This prevents air from drying out your food and helps retain moisture and flavour. Glass containers are great for this, as they're easy to clean, stack well in the fridge, and can go straight into the air fryer for reheating.

- **Tip 2: Label and Date Your Leftovers**

  If you're someone who cooks in bulk, it's easy to lose track of what's been in the fridge for a while. Always label and date your containers so you know exactly when they were cooked. As a rule of thumb, most cooked foods can last in the fridge for about 3-5 days.

- **Tip 3: Freeze When Necessary**

  For meals you won't eat right away, freezing is your best bet. Make sure to use freezer-safe containers or bags and label them with the date. When freezing, leave a little room at the top of the container to allow for expansion, especially with liquids like soups or stews.

2. How to Reheat Food in the Ninja Air Fryer

When it's time to enjoy your leftovers, the Ninja Air Fryer is your best friend. It's not just about heating food up—it's about re-crisping and rejuvenating your meal, so it tastes just as good as it did the first time.

- **Tip 1: Reheat with the Air Fry or Reheat Setting**

  The Ninja Air Fryer has a Reheat setting, which is perfect for warming up most leftovers without drying them out. However, for crispy foods like pizza, fries, or chicken wings, the Air Fry setting is a better option to bring back that golden crunch.

- **Tip 2: Use Lower Temperatures for Reheating**

  Unlike cooking from scratch, reheating doesn't require high temperatures. Set your air fryer to a lower temperature—around 150°C (300°F)—and reheat for 3-5 minutes, depending on the food. For items like pizza or fries, you can crank it up to 180°C (350°F) for a minute or two at the end to restore crispiness.

- **Tip 3: Don't Overcrowd the Basket**

  When reheating food, avoid overcrowding the air fryer basket. Spread out the food in a single layer so the hot air can circulate around it evenly. If you're reheating larger quantities, it's better to do it in batches for the best results.

- **Tip 4: Add Moisture to Dry Foods**

Some foods, like pasta or rice, can dry out in the fridge. To avoid this, sprinkle a little water over the food before reheating. For dishes like casseroles or pasta bakes, covering the top with foil for the first few minutes will help retain moisture.

3. Reheating Specific Foods: Best Practices

Let's take a look at how to reheat different types of leftovers to ensure they taste just as good as they did when you first made them.

Reheating Pizza:

Pizza is notoriously difficult to reheat in the microwave—it often ends up soggy or chewy. With the Ninja Air Fryer, you can restore that crispy crust and gooey cheese in minutes. Set the air fryer to 180°C (350°F) and reheat for about 3-5 minutes. If the pizza has extra toppings, you might want to cover it with foil for the first couple of minutes to prevent the toppings from overcooking.

Reheating Fries and Fried Foods:

Fries and fried foods tend to lose their crispiness when stored, but the air fryer brings them back to life. Use the Air Fry setting at 190°C (375°F) for about 3-4 minutes. Shake the basket halfway through for even crisping, and your fries or chicken tenders will taste freshly made.

Reheating Rice and Pasta:

Rice and pasta can dry out in the fridge, but a little moisture can fix that. Sprinkle a few drops of water over the rice or pasta, then set the air fryer to 150°C (300°F) and reheat for about 3-5 minutes. Cover with foil if necessary to trap steam and prevent it from drying out further.

Reheating Roasted Vegetables:

Roasted veggies tend to lose their crisp texture after being stored in the fridge. To re-crisp them, use the Air Fry or Reheat setting at 180°C (350°F) for about 4-5 minutes, shaking the basket halfway through. You'll have crispy, caramelised veggies just like when they were first roasted.

Reheating Meats:

For reheating meat like chicken breasts, steak, or pork chops, use the Reheat setting at 160°C (320°F) for about 4-6 minutes, depending on the size of the portions. You can switch to Air Fry for the last minute if you want to crisp up the edges or skin.

4. Making the Most of Leftovers: Creative Ideas

Sometimes reheating leftovers as-is can feel a bit boring, so why not get creative? The Ninja Air Fryer makes it easy to transform yesterday's meal into something new and exciting.

- **Tip 1: Turn Leftover Veggies into Frittatas**

  If you've got leftover roasted vegetables, toss them into a frittata or quiche. Just whisk up some eggs, mix in the veggies, and use the Bake setting on your air fryer to cook it through. In 10-15 minutes, you'll have a delicious frittata for breakfast or lunch.

- **Tip 2: Use Leftover Meat for Wraps or Salads**

  Leftover grilled chicken or beef can be quickly transformed into a fresh meal by adding it to a wrap or salad. Reheat the meat using the Reheat function, slice it up, and toss it with your favourite veggies, cheeses, or sauces.

- **Tip 3: Revamp Stale Bread into Croutons**

  Got stale bread? Don't throw it away—turn it into crispy croutons using the air fryer! Cube the bread, toss it with olive oil, garlic, and herbs, and air-fry at 180°C (350°F) for about 5 minutes. You'll have golden croutons perfect for soups and salads.

EXCLUSIVE BONUS

40 Weight Loss Recipes

&

14 Days Meal Plan

Scan the QR-Code and receive
the FREE download:

CHAPTER 1:
BREAKFAST AND BRUNCH

AIR-CRISPED HASH BROWNS

Golden and crispy hash browns, perfect for a classic British breakfast.

Portions: 4 | **Difficulty Level:** Easy | **Preparation Time:** 10 minutes |
Cooking Time: 20 minutes | **Total Time:** 30 minutes

INGREDIENTS:

- 500 g potatoes, peeled and grated
- 1 small onion, grated
- 1 tablespoon olive oil
- 1 teaspoon salt
- 1/2 teaspoon freshly ground black pepper
- 1/2 teaspoon paprika (optional)

ESTIMATED NUTRITIONAL INFORMATION PER SERVING:
Calories: approx. 200 kcal | Fat: approx. 6 g | Carbohydrates: approx. 30 g |
Protein: approx. 3 g | Salt: approx. 0.8 g

INSTRUCTIONS:

1. **Prepare the potatoes:** After grating the potatoes, place them in a clean kitchen towel and squeeze out as much moisture as possible. Combine the grated potatoes, grated onion, olive oil, salt, pepper, and paprika in a large bowl, mixing well.
2. **Shape the hash browns:** Divide the potato mixture into small portions and shape them into patties, about 1 cm thick.
3. **Preheat the air fryer:** Set your Ninja Air Fryer to the Air Crisp setting at 200°C (390°F). Preheat for 3 minutes.
4. **Cook the hash browns:** Place the hash brown patties in the air fryer basket in a single layer, making sure they don't overlap. Air-crisp for 10 minutes, then flip them and cook for another 10 minutes until golden and crispy. For extra crispiness, you can add an additional 3-4 minutes of cooking time.
5. **Serve:** Remove the hash browns from the air fryer and serve hot with eggs, bacon, or your favourite breakfast sides. They're also great with a dollop of ketchup or HP sauce.

EGG AND BACON BREAKFAST MUFFINS

Savoury muffins filled with bacon and egg, cooked in the Bake function.

Portions: 6 muffins | **Difficulty Level:** Easy | **Preparation Time:** 10 minutes | **Cooking Time**: 15 minutes | **Total Time:** 25 minutes

INGREDIENTS:

- 6 slices of bacon
- 6 large eggs
- 50 g cheddar cheese, grated
- 1 tablespoon fresh chives, chopped
- Salt and freshly ground black pepper to taste
- 1 tablespoon olive oil (optional, for greasing the muffin tin)

ESTIMATED NUTRITIONAL INFORMATION PER MUFFIN:
Calories: approx. 160 kcal | Fat: approx. 12 g | Carbohydrates: approx. 1 g | Protein: approx. 10 g | Salt: approx. 0.6 g

INSTRUCTIONS:

1. **Cook the bacon:** Set your Ninja Air Fryer to the Bake setting at 180°C (350°F). Place the bacon slices in the air fryer basket and cook for 5-6 minutes, or until crispy. Remove the bacon and set aside on a paper towel to drain. Once cool, chop the bacon into small pieces.
2. **Prepare the muffin tin:** Lightly grease a silicone muffin tray or metal muffin tin with olive oil. You can also use muffin liners for easier cleanup.
3. **Assemble the muffins:** Crack one egg into each muffin cup. Top each egg with a handful of grated cheddar cheese, the chopped bacon, and a sprinkle of fresh chives. Season each muffin with salt and pepper.
4. **Bake the muffins:** Place the muffin tin in the air fryer and bake at 180°C (350°F) for 12-15 minutes, or until the eggs are set and the cheese is melted. For a runny yolk, reduce the cooking time to 10 minutes.
5. **Serve:** Let the muffins cool for a few minutes before removing them from the tin. Serve hot, alongside toast or as a grab-and-go breakfast option.

SAUSAGE AND BEAN BREAKFAST WRAPS

Savoury sausages and baked beans wrapped in tortillas and air-crisped for a delicious breakfast on the go.

Portions: 4 wraps | **Difficulty Level:** Easy | **Preparation Time:** 10 minutes | **Cooking Time**: 12 minutes | **Total Time:** 22 minutes

INGREDIENTS:

- 4 sausages (pork or vegetarian)
- 1 can (400 g) baked beans
- 4 large tortillas
- 100 g cheddar cheese, grated
- 1 tablespoon olive oil
- Salt and freshly ground black pepper to taste

ESTIMATED NUTRITIONAL INFORMATION PER WRAP:
Calories: approx. 350 kcal | Fat: approx. 15 g | Carbohydrates: approx. 35 g | Protein: approx. 15 g | Salt: approx. 1.2 g

INSTRUCTIONS:

1. **Cook the sausages:** Preheat the Ninja Air Fryer to the Air Crisp setting at 200°C (390°F). Place the sausages in the air fryer basket and cook for 10 minutes, turning halfway through. Once cooked, remove the sausages and slice them into pieces.
2. **Warm the beans:** While the sausages cook, heat the baked beans in a small saucepan or in the microwave until warmed through.
3. **Assemble the wraps:** Lay out the tortillas and spread a spoonful of baked beans onto each one. Top with sliced sausages and a handful of grated cheddar cheese. Season with salt and pepper.
4. **Wrap the tortillas:** Fold the sides of each tortilla inward, then roll them up to form a wrap. Brush each wrap lightly with olive oil to ensure they crisp up in the air fryer.
5. **Crisp the wraps:** Place the wraps in the air fryer basket and air-crisp at 180°C (350°F) for 5-7 minutes, or until the tortillas are golden and crispy.
6. **Serve:** Serve the wraps hot, with a side of extra baked beans or ketchup for dipping. These wraps make for a hearty breakfast or a quick lunch.

VEGETARIAN BREAKFAST BURRITOS

Packed with scrambled eggs, beans, and veggies, these breakfast burritos are air-crisped until golden for a hearty and delicious start to the day.

Portions: 4 burritos | **Difficulty Level:** Easy | **Preparation Time:** 10 minutes | **Cooking Time:** 10 minutes | **Total Time:** 20 minutes

INGREDIENTS:

- 6 large eggs
- 1 small onion, diced
- 1 small red bell pepper, diced
- 100 g black beans, drained and rinsed
- 100 g cheddar cheese, grated
- 4 large tortillas
- 1 tablespoon olive oil

- 1 teaspoon ground cumin
- Salt and freshly ground black pepper to taste
- 1 tablespoon fresh coriander, chopped (optional)
- Salsa and sour cream for serving (optional)

ESTIMATED NUTRITIONAL INFORMATION PER BURRITO:
Calories: approx. 320 kcal | Fat: approx. 15 g | Carbohydrates: approx. 30 g | Protein: approx. 16 g | Salt: approx. 1.0 g

INSTRUCTIONS:

1. **Scramble the eggs:** In a large frying-pan, heat 1 tablespoon of olive oil over medium heat. Add the diced onion and red bell pepper, sautéing for 3-4 minutes until softened. Add the eggs to the pan and season with cumin, salt, and pepper. Stir until the eggs are scrambled and cooked through. Remove from heat and stir in the black beans and fresh coriander.
2. **Assemble the burritos:** Lay the tortillas flat and divide the egg mixture evenly among them. Top each with a handful of grated cheddar cheese. Roll up the tortillas by folding in the sides and rolling them tightly.
3. **Crisp the burritos:** Preheat your Ninja Air Fryer to the Air Crisp setting at 180°C (350°F). Lightly brush the burritos with olive oil and place them in the air fryer basket, seam side down. Air-crisp for 5-7 minutes until the burritos are golden and crispy.
4. **Serve:** Serve the burritos hot, with salsa and sour cream on the side. These breakfast burritos are perfect for a quick meal on the go.

GRILLED KIPPERS WITH LEMON AND BUTTER

A traditional British breakfast staple, kippers are perfectly grilled in the Ninja Air Fryer and finished with a squeeze of lemon and a pat of butter.

Portions: 2 | **Difficulty Level:** Easy | **Preparation Time:** 5 minutes | **Cooking Time**: 8 minutes | **Total Time:** 13 minutes

INGREDIENTS:

- 2 whole kippers, cleaned and deboned
- 1 tablespoon butter
- 1 tablespoon olive oil
- 1 lemon, halved
- Freshly ground black pepper to taste
- Fresh parsley for garnish (optional)

ESTIMATED NUTRITIONAL INFORMATION PER SERVING:
Calories: approx. 200 kcal | Fat: approx. 14 g | Carbohydrates: approx. 2 g | Protein: approx. 18 g | Salt: approx. 0.8 g

INSTRUCTIONS:

1. **Prepare the** kippers: Preheat your Ninja Air Fryer to the Grill setting at 180°C (350°F). Brush the kippers with olive oil and season with black pepper.
2. **Grill the kippers:** Place the kippers in the air fryer basket and grill for 7-8 minutes, or until the fish is cooked through and slightly crispy on the edges.
3. **Add butter and lemon:** Once cooked, remove the kippers from the air fryer. While they are still hot, add a pat of butter to each fish and squeeze fresh lemon juice over the top.
4. **Serve:** Serve the grilled kippers with additional lemon wedges and a sprinkle of fresh parsley for garnish. These kippers pair perfectly with toast and eggs for a complete breakfast.

EGGS AND SOLDIERS ON TOAST

Classic soft-boiled eggs served with crispy toast soldiers, air-fried to perfection for a delicious British breakfast.

Portions: 2 | **Difficulty Level:** Easy | **Preparation Time:** 5 minutes |
Cooking Time: 8 minutes | **Total Time:** 13 minutes

INGREDIENTS:

- 4 large eggs
- 4 slices of bread (white or wholemeal)
- 2 tablespoons butter
- Salt and freshly ground black pepper to taste

ESTIMATED NUTRITIONAL INFORMATION PER SERVING:
Calories: approx. 250 kcal | Fat: approx. 14 g | Carbohydrates: approx. 20 g |
Protein: approx. 12 g | Salt: approx. 0.6 g

INSTRUCTIONS:

1. **Cook the eggs:** Preheat the Ninja Air Fryer to 120°C (250°F) on the Bake setting. Place the eggs in the air fryer basket and bake for 8 minutes for soft-boiled eggs. For medium-boiled eggs, increase the cooking time by 2-3 minutes.

2. **Prepare the toast soldiers:** While the eggs cook, spread the butter on both sides of the bread slices. Place the buttered bread in the air fryer basket and air-crisp at 180°C (350°F) for 3-4 minutes, or until golden and crispy. Once toasted, cut each slice into strips (soldiers).

3. **Serve:** Place the soft-boiled eggs in egg cups and serve with the crispy toast soldiers on the side. Season the eggs with salt and freshly ground black pepper for extra flavour.

BREAKFAST POTATO WEDGES

Golden and crispy potato wedges, seasoned to perfection and air-crisped for a delicious breakfast side.

Portions: 4 | **Difficulty Level:** Easy | **Preparation Time:** 10 minutes | **Cooking Time**: 20 minutes | **Total Time:** 30 minutes

INGREDIENTS:

- 500 g potatoes, cut into wedges
- 1 tablespoon olive oil
- 1 teaspoon smoked paprika
- 1/2 teaspoon garlic powder
- Salt and freshly ground black pepper to taste
- Fresh parsley, chopped (optional)

ESTIMATED NUTRITIONAL INFORMATION PER SERVING:
Calories: approx. 180 kcal | Fat: approx. 6 g | Carbohydrates: approx. 30 g | Protein: approx. 3 g | Salt: approx. 0.8 g

INSTRUCTIONS:

1. **Prepare the potatoes:** Preheat the Ninja Air Fryer to the Air Crisp setting at 200°C (390°F). In a large bowl, toss the potato wedges with olive oil, smoked paprika, garlic powder, salt, and pepper until evenly coated.
2. **Air-crisp the potatoes:** Place the seasoned potato wedges in the air fryer basket in a single layer. Air-crisp for 18-20 minutes, shaking the basket halfway through cooking to ensure even crisping.
3. **Check for doneness:** The wedges should be golden brown and crispy on the outside, while tender on the inside. If needed, add an additional 2-3 minutes for extra crispiness.
4. **Serve:** Transfer the crispy wedges to a serving plate and garnish with fresh parsley if desired. Serve hot with scrambled eggs, bacon, or your favourite breakfast main.

MUSHROOM AND SPINACH FRITTATA

A savoury frittata made with mushrooms, spinach, and cheese, cooked to perfection using the Bake function of the Ninja Air Fryer.

Portions: 4 | **Difficulty Level:** Easy | **Preparation Time:** 10 minutes |
Cooking Time: 15 minutes | **Total Time:** 25 minutes

INGREDIENTS:

- 6 large eggs
- 100 g fresh spinach, chopped
- 100 g mushrooms, sliced
- 50 g cheddar cheese, grated
- 1 small onion, finely chopped
- 2 tablespoons olive oil
- Salt and freshly ground black pepper to taste

ESTIMATED NUTRITIONAL INFORMATION PER SERVING:
Calories: approx. 450 kcal | Fat: approx. 30 g | Carbohydrates: approx. 20 g | Protein: approx. 25 g | Salt: approx. 2.0 g

INSTRUCTIONS:

1. **Sauté the vegetables:** Preheat the Ninja Air Fryer to the Bake setting at 180°C (350°F). In a frying-pan, heat 1 tablespoon of olive oil over medium heat. Sauté the onion and mushrooms for 3-4 minutes until softened. Add the spinach and cook for another 2 minutes until wilted. Remove from heat and set aside.

2. **Prepare the frittata:** In a large bowl, whisk the eggs and season with salt and black pepper. Stir in the sautéed vegetables and half of the grated cheddar cheese.

3. **Bake the frittata:** Lightly grease an air fryer-safe baking dish with the remaining olive oil. Pour the egg mixture into the dish and sprinkle the remaining cheddar cheese on top. Place the dish in the air fryer and bake for 12-15 minutes, or until the frittata is set and the top is golden.

4. **Serve:** Let the frittata cool slightly before slicing. Serve hot with a side of toast or a light salad for a complete breakfast or brunch.

FULL ENGLISH BREAKFAST TRAY

A complete Full English breakfast made all at once in the Ninja Air Fryer, featuring sausages, bacon, eggs, mushrooms, tomatoes, and toast.

Portions: 2 | **Difficulty Level:** Medium | **Preparation Time:** 10 minutes | **Cooking Time**: 15 minutes | **Total Time:** 25 minutes

INGREDIENTS:

- 2 sausages (pork or vegetarian)
- 2 slices of bacon
- 4 mushrooms, sliced
- 2 tomatoes, halved
- 2 eggs
- 2 slices of bread
- 1 tablespoon olive oil
- Salt and freshly ground black pepper to taste
- Baked beans (optional)

ESTIMATED NUTRITIONAL INFORMATION PER SERVING:
Calories: approx. 450 kcal | Fat: approx. 30 g | Carbohydrates: approx. 20 g | Protein: approx. 25 g | Salt: approx. 2.0 g

INSTRUCTIONS:

1. **Prepare the ingredients:** Preheat the Ninja Air Fryer to the Air Crisp setting at 200°C (390°F). Lightly brush the tomatoes and mushrooms with olive oil and season with salt and pepper.
2. **Cook the sausages and bacon:** Place the sausages and bacon in the air fryer basket. Air-crisp for 5 minutes, then flip the sausages and bacon.
3. **Add the vegetables:** After 5 minutes of cooking the sausages and bacon, add the halved tomatoes and sliced mushrooms to the air fryer basket. Continue cooking for another 5 minutes.
4. **Cook the eggs and toast:** Once the sausages, bacon, and vegetables are nearly done, crack the eggs into individual ramekins or small oven-safe dishes. Place the eggs and slices of bread in the air fryer basket. Air-crisp for 3-4 minutes, until the eggs are cooked to your liking and the bread is toasted.
5. **Serve:** Plate the sausages, bacon, mushrooms, tomatoes, eggs, and toast. Serve with baked beans on the side if desired.

BLUEBERRY PANCAKES

Fluffy pancakes cooked in the air fryer's Bake setting, served with fresh blueberries and maple syrup for a delicious start to the day.

Portions: 4 | **Difficulty Level:** Easy | **Preparation Time:** 10 minutes |
Cooking Time: 10 minutes | **Total Time:** 20 minutes

INGREDIENTS:

- 150 g plain flour
- 1 tablespoon sugar
- 1 teaspoon baking powder
- 1/2 teaspoon baking soda
- 1/4 teaspoon salt
- 250 ml milk
- 1 large egg
- 1 tablespoon melted butter (plus extra for greasing)
- 100 g fresh blueberries
- Maple syrup (for serving)

ESTIMATED NUTRITIONAL INFORMATION PER SERVING:
Calories: approx. 220 kcal | Fat: approx. 8 g | Carbohydrates: approx. 30 g |
Protein: approx. 6 g | Salt: approx. 0.5 g

INSTRUCTIONS:

1. **Prepare the batter:** In a large bowl, whisk together the flour, sugar, baking powder, baking soda, and salt. In a separate bowl, whisk the milk, egg, and melted butter until well combined. Gradually add the wet ingredients to the dry ingredients, whisking until smooth. Gently fold in the fresh blueberries.
2. **Preheat the air fryer:** Preheat your Ninja Air Fryer to the Bake setting at 180°C (350°F). Lightly grease a small air fryer-safe baking dish with butter.
3. **Cook the pancakes:** Pour a portion of the batter into the greased baking dish, spreading it evenly. Bake for 8-10 minutes until the pancake is puffed and golden on top. Use a spatula to carefully remove the pancake from the dish. Repeat with the remaining batter.
4. **Serve:** Serve the pancakes hot, drizzled with maple syrup and extra blueberries. These pancakes pair perfectly with a side of bacon or sausage for a complete breakfast.

CRISPY BACON BUTTIES

Bacon air-crisped until golden, served in a traditional British butty with a generous spread of butter.

Portions: 2 | **Difficulty Level:** Easy | **Preparation Time:** 5 minutes | **Cooking Time**: 10 minutes | **Total Time:** 15 minutes

INGREDIENTS:

- 4 rashers of bacon
- 4 slices of white or wholemeal bread
- 2 tablespoons butter
- Salt and freshly ground black pepper to taste
- Tomato ketchup or brown sauce (optional)

ESTIMATED NUTRITIONAL INFORMATION PER SERVING:
Calories: approx. 350 kcal | Fat: approx. 20 g | Carbohydrates: approx. 30 g | Protein: approx. 12 g | Salt: approx. 1.5 g

INSTRUCTIONS:

1. **Cook the bacon:** Preheat your Ninja Air Fryer to the Air Crisp setting at 200°C (390°F). Lay the bacon rashers in the air fryer basket in a single layer and air-crisp for 8-10 minutes, flipping halfway through, until crispy and golden.
2. **Prepare the butties:** While the bacon is cooking, butter the slices of bread generously.
3. **Assemble the butties:** Once the bacon is crispy, remove it from the air fryer and place two rashers on each buttered slice of bread. Season with salt and pepper to taste. Add ketchup or brown sauce if desired.
4. **Serve:** Cut the butties in half and serve hot. These bacon butties are perfect for a quick, satisfying breakfast or lunch.

SAVOURY OATCAKES WITH CHEESE AND CHIVES

Traditional British-style oatcakes baked with cheddar cheese and fresh chives, perfect for a savoury breakfast or snack.

Portions: 4 | **Difficulty Level:** Easy | **Preparation Time:** 10 minutes | **Cooking Time**: 12 minutes | **Total Time:** 22 minutes

INGREDIENTS:

- 100 g rolled oats
- 50 g plain flour
- 50 g cheddar cheese, grated
- 2 tablespoons fresh chives, chopped
- 50 ml water
- 2 tablespoons olive oil
- 1/2 teaspoon baking powder
- Salt and freshly ground black pepper to taste

ESTIMATED NUTRITIONAL INFORMATION PER SERVING:
Calories: approx. 180 kcal | Fat: approx. 9 g | Carbohydrates: approx. 20 g | Protein: approx. 5 g | Salt: approx. 0.5 g

INSTRUCTIONS:

1. **Prepare the dough:** In a large bowl, mix the rolled oats, flour, cheddar cheese, chopped chives, baking powder, salt, and pepper. Add the olive oil and water, mixing until a dough forms.
2. **Shape the oatcakes:** Preheat your Ninja Air Fryer to the Bake setting at 180°C (350°F). Divide the dough into 8 equal portions and shape each portion into a small, flat round oatcake, about 1 cm thick.
3. **Bake the oatcakes:** Place the oatcakes in the air fryer basket in a single layer and bake for 10-12 minutes, or until golden and crisp on the edges.
4. **Serve:** Serve the savoury oatcakes warm, with extra cheese or butter if desired. They make a great addition to a traditional British breakfast or can be enjoyed on their own as a snack.

SCOTCH PANCAKES WITH HONEY

Small, fluffy Scotch pancakes drizzled with honey for a sweet and simple breakfast or snack.

Portions: 4 | **Difficulty Level:** Easy | **Preparation Time:** 5 minutes |
Cooking Time: 10 minutes | **Total Time:** 15 minutes

INGREDIENTS:

- 150 g self-raising flour
- 1 tablespoon sugar
- 1/2 teaspoon baking powder
- 1 large egg
- 150 ml milk
- 1 tablespoon butter (plus extra for greasing)
- Honey, for drizzling

ESTIMATED NUTRITIONAL INFORMATION PER SERVING:
Calories: approx. 220 kcal | Fat: approx. 8 g | Carbohydrates: approx. 30 g |
Protein: approx. 5 g | Salt: approx. 0.3 g

INSTRUCTIONS:

1. **Prepare the batter:** In a large bowl, mix the flour, sugar, and baking powder. In a separate bowl, whisk together the egg and milk. Gradually add the wet ingredients to the dry ingredients, whisking until smooth.
2. **Preheat the air fryer:** Preheat your Ninja Air Fryer to the Bake setting at 180°C (350°F). Lightly grease a small air fryer-safe baking dish or mould with butter.
3. **Cook the pancakes:** Spoon small amounts of the batter into the greased baking dish to form mini pancakes. Bake for 8-10 minutes, or until the pancakes are fluffy and lightly golden.
4. **Serve:** Stack the pancakes on a plate and drizzle generously with honey. These Scotch pancakes are perfect for breakfast or a light afternoon snack.

AIR-FRIED BREAKFAST CROISSANTS

Golden croissants filled with ham and cheese, air-baked to perfection for a delightful breakfast.

Portions: 4 | **Difficulty Level:** Easy | **Preparation Time:** 5 minutes | **Cooking Time:** 8 minutes | **Total Time:** 13 minutes

INGREDIENTS:

- 4 pre-made croissant doughs (or ready-to-bake croissants)
- 4 slices of ham
- 50 g cheddar cheese, grated
- 1 tablespoon butter (optional, for brushing)

ESTIMATED NUTRITIONAL INFORMATION PER SERVING:
Calories: approx. 280 kcal | Fat: approx. 15 g | Carbohydrates: approx. 20 g | Protein: approx. 12 g | Salt: approx. 1.0 g

INSTRUCTIONS:

1. **Assemble the croissants:** Preheat the Ninja Air Fryer to the Bake setting at 180°C (350°F). Unroll the croissant dough and place a slice of ham and a sprinkle of grated cheese on each piece. Roll them up into croissant shapes.
2. **Brush with butter (optional):** If desired, lightly brush the tops of the croissants with melted butter for extra golden crispiness.
3. **Bake the croissants:** Place the croissants in the air fryer basket in a single layer, ensuring they have enough space to rise. Bake for 6-8 minutes until they are golden brown and the cheese is melted.
4. **Serve:** Serve the croissants hot for a warm, cheesy breakfast. Pair with fresh fruit or a cup of coffee for a complete breakfast experience.

TOMATO AND CHEESE BREAKFAST BAKE

A hearty breakfast casserole with eggs, cheese, and tomatoes, baked to perfection in the Ninja Air Fryer.

Portions: 4 | **Difficulty Level:** Easy | **Preparation Time:** 10 minutes | **Cooking Time**: 15 minutes | **Total Time:** 25 minutes

INGREDIENTS:

- 4 large eggs
- 150 g cherry tomatoes, halved
- 100 g cheddar cheese, grated
- 1 small onion, finely chopped
- 1 tablespoon olive oil
- Salt and freshly ground black pepper to taste
- Fresh parsley for garnish (optional)

ESTIMATED NUTRITIONAL INFORMATION PER SERVING:
Calories: approx. 220 kcal | Fat: approx. 16 g | Carbohydrates: approx. 4 g | Protein: approx. 13 g | Salt: approx. 0.8 g

INSTRUCTIONS:

1. **Prepare the vegetables:** Preheat the Ninja Air Fryer to the Bake setting at 180°C (350°F). In a frying-pan, heat the olive oil over medium heat and sauté the onion for 3-4 minutes until softened. Add the halved cherry tomatoes and cook for another 2 minutes. Remove from heat.
2. **Assemble the bake:** In a large bowl, whisk the eggs and season with salt and black pepper. Stir in the sautéed vegetables and half of the grated cheddar cheese.
3. **Bake the casserole:** Lightly grease an air fryer-safe baking dish and pour the egg mixture into the dish. Sprinkle the remaining cheddar cheese on top. Place the dish in the air fryer and bake for 12-15 minutes, or until the eggs are set and the cheese is golden.
4. **Serve:** Garnish with fresh parsley if desired and serve hot. This breakfast bake is perfect on its own or paired with toast for a complete breakfast.

CHAPTER 2:
STARTERS AND SNACKS

CRISPY CHICKPEA BITES

Seasoned and air-crisped chickpeas, perfect for a healthy and crunchy snack or starter.

Portions: 4 | **Difficulty Level:** Easy | **Preparation Time:** 5 minutes | **Cooking Time**: 15 minutes | **Total Time:** 20 minutes

INGREDIENTS:

- 1 can (400 g) chickpeas, drained and rinsed
- 1 tablespoon olive oil
- 1 teaspoon smoked paprika
- 1/2 teaspoon garlic powder
- Salt and freshly ground black pepper to taste
- Fresh parsley, chopped (optional, for garnish)

ESTIMATED NUTRITIONAL INFORMATION PER SERVING:
Calories: approx. 130 kcal | Fat: approx. 5 g | Carbohydrates: approx. 15 g | Protein: approx. 5 g | Salt: approx. 0.6 g

INSTRUCTIONS:

1. **Prepare the chickpeas:** Preheat your Ninja Air Fryer to the Air Crisp setting at 200°C (390°F). Pat the drained chickpeas dry with a clean kitchen towel. In a bowl, toss the chickpeas with olive oil, smoked paprika, garlic powder, salt, and black pepper.
2. **Air-crisp the chickpeas:** Spread the chickpeas in the air fryer basket in a single layer. Air-crisp for 12-15 minutes, shaking the basket halfway through to ensure even crisping. The chickpeas should be golden and crunchy.
3. **Serve:** Transfer the crispy chickpeas to a serving bowl and garnish with fresh parsley if desired. These chickpea bites are perfect as a snack or a healthy appetiser with a dip.

STUFFED MINI PEPPERS WITH CREAM CHEESE

Colourful mini peppers stuffed with a creamy herb cheese filling, air-crisped until golden for a delightful snack or starter.

Portions: 4 | **Difficulty Level:** Easy | **Preparation Time:** 10 minutes | **Cooking Time**: 8 minutes | **Total Time:** 18 minutes

INGREDIENTS:

- 12 mini sweet peppers, halved and deseeded
- 150 g cream cheese
- 2 tablespoons fresh chives, chopped
- 1 tablespoon fresh parsley, chopped
- 1 clove garlic, minced
- 1 tablespoon olive oil
- Salt and freshly ground black pepper to taste

ESTIMATED NUTRITIONAL INFORMATION PER SERVING:
Calories: approx. 120 kcal | Fat: approx. 10 g | Carbohydrates: approx. 5 g | Protein: approx. 2 g | Salt: approx. 0.5 g

INSTRUCTIONS:

1. **Prepare the filling:** In a bowl, mix together the cream cheese, chives, parsley, minced garlic, salt, and black pepper until well combined.
2. **Stuff the peppers:** Preheat your Ninja Air Fryer to the Air Crisp setting at 180°C (350°F). Spoon the cream cheese mixture into the halved mini peppers.
3. **Air-crisp the peppers:** Lightly brush the tops of the stuffed peppers with olive oil and place them in the air fryer basket in a single layer. Air-crisp for 6-8 minutes, or until the peppers are tender and the tops are lightly golden.
4. **Serve:** Serve the stuffed peppers hot as an appetiser or snack. They can be garnished with extra herbs for a fresh finish.

VEGETARIAN SAUSAGE ROLLS

Flaky pastry rolls stuffed with a plant-based sausage filling, air-crisped to golden perfection for a delicious snack or starter.

Portions: 4 | **Difficulty Level:** Easy | **Preparation Time:** 10 minutes | **Cooking Time**: 12 minutes | **Total Time:** 22 minutes

INGREDIENTS:

- 4 vegetarian sausages
- 1 sheet of puff pastry (ready-made)
- 1 tablespoon Dijon mustard
- 1 egg, beaten (for glazing)
- 1 teaspoon sesame seeds (optional, for garnish)
- Salt and freshly ground black pepper to taste

ESTIMATED NUTRITIONAL INFORMATION PER SERVING:
Calories: approx. 250 kcal | Fat: approx. 15 g | Carbohydrates: approx. 20 g | Protein: approx. 6 g | Salt: approx. 1.0 g

INSTRUCTIONS:

1. **Prepare the sausage rolls:** Preheat your Ninja Air Fryer to the Air Crisp setting at 190°C (375°F). Unroll the puff pastry sheet and cut it into 4 equal rectangles. Spread a thin layer of Dijon mustard on each rectangle of pastry.
2. **Assemble the rolls:** Place one vegetarian sausage in the centre of each pastry rectangle. Fold the pastry over the sausage, sealing the edges by pressing with your fingers. Brush the top of each roll with the beaten egg and sprinkle with sesame seeds, if desired.
3. **Air-crisp the rolls:** Place the sausage rolls in the air fryer basket, seam side down, ensuring they don't touch. Air-crisp for 10-12 minutes until the pastry is golden and puffed.
4. **Serve:** Remove the sausage rolls from the air fryer and let them cool slightly before serving. These vegetarian sausage rolls make a great snack or light meal.

CRISPY HALLOUMI FRIES

Golden and crispy halloumi sticks, air-fried to perfection and served with a fresh dip for a savoury snack or starter.

Portions: 4 | **Difficulty Level:** Easy | **Preparation Time:** 5 minutes | **Cooking Time**: 10 minutes | **Total Time:** 15 minutes

INGREDIENTS:

- 250 g halloumi cheese, cut into sticks
- 2 tablespoons plain flour
- 1 tablespoon olive oil
- 1 teaspoon smoked paprika
- Fresh parsley, chopped (optional, for garnish)
- Lemon wedges for serving

ESTIMATED NUTRITIONAL INFORMATION PER SERVING:
Calories: approx. 220 kcal | Fat: approx. 18 g | Carbohydrates: approx. 5 g | Protein: approx. 10 g | Salt: approx. 1.5 g

INSTRUCTIONS:

1. **Prepare the halloumi:** Preheat the Ninja Air Fryer to the Air Crisp setting at 200°C (390°F). In a small bowl, toss the halloumi sticks with the flour and smoked paprika, ensuring they are evenly coated.
2. **Air-crisp the halloumi:** Lightly brush the halloumi sticks with olive oil. Place the halloumi sticks in the air fryer basket in a single layer, ensuring they don't overlap. Air-crisp for 8-10 minutes, turning halfway through, until golden and crispy on the outside.
3. **Serve:** Transfer the crispy halloumi fries to a serving plate and garnish with fresh parsley. Serve with lemon wedges on the side for a fresh, tangy flavour. These halloumi fries pair perfectly with a garlic or yoghourt dip.

PRAWN TOAST

A healthier version of the classic prawn toast, air-crisped for a crunchy, golden finish, perfect as a snack or starter.

Portions: 4 | **Difficulty Level:** Medium | **Preparation Time:** 10 minutes | **Cooking Time**: 10 minutes | **Total Time:** 20 minutes

INGREDIENTS:

- 200 g prawns, peeled and deveined
- 1 clove garlic, minced
- 1 tablespoon soy sauce
- 1 teaspoon sesame oil
- 2 slices of white bread, crusts removed
- 1 tablespoon sesame seeds
- 1 tablespoon vegetable oil (for brushing)
- Fresh coriander for garnish (optional)

ESTIMATED NUTRITIONAL INFORMATION PER SERVING:
Calories: approx. 150 kcal | Fat: approx. 8 g | Carbohydrates: approx. 10 g | Protein: approx. 10 g | Salt: approx. 0.7 g

INSTRUCTIONS:

1. **Prepare the prawn mixture:** In a food processor, blend the prawns, garlic, soy sauce, and sesame oil until you have a smooth paste.
2. **Assemble the prawn toasts:** Spread the prawn mixture evenly over each slice of bread. Cut each slice of bread into 4 triangles. Sprinkle sesame seeds over the top of the prawn mixture and lightly press them in.
3. **Air-crisp the prawn toasts:** Preheat the Ninja Air Fryer to the Air Crisp setting at 180°C (350°F). Lightly brush the tops of the prawn toasts with vegetable oil. Place the toasts in the air fryer basket in a single layer, prawn-side up, and air-crisp for 8-10 minutes until golden and crispy.
4. **Serve:** Serve the prawn toasts hot, garnished with fresh coriander if desired. These toasts are delicious on their own or served with a dipping sauce like sweet chilli.

AIR-FRIED ONION BHAJIS

A healthier take on the classic Indian snack, these onion bhajis are air-crisped to golden perfection and packed with flavour.

Portions: 4 | **Difficulty Level:** Medium | **Preparation Time:** 10 minutes | **Cooking Time**: 12 minutes | **Total Time:** 22 minutes

INGREDIENTS:

- 2 medium onions, thinly sliced
- 100 g gram (chickpea) flour
- 1 teaspoon ground cumin
- 1 teaspoon ground coriander
- 1/2 teaspoon turmeric powder
- 1/2 teaspoon chilli powder

- 1/2 teaspoon baking powder
- 1 tablespoon fresh coriander, chopped
- 1 tablespoon lemon juice
- 1 tablespoon vegetable oil (for brushing)
- Salt to taste

ESTIMATED NUTRITIONAL INFORMATION PER SERVING:
Calories: approx. 180 kcal | Fat: approx. 6 g | Carbohydrates: approx. 24 g | Protein: approx. 5 g | Salt: approx. 0.5 g

INSTRUCTIONS:

1. **Prepare the batter:** In a large bowl, mix the gram flour, cumin, coriander, turmeric, chilli powder, baking powder, and salt. Add the sliced onions, fresh coriander, and lemon juice. Slowly add water, about 50 ml at a time, stirring until you have a thick batter that coats the onions.
2. **Shape the bhajis:** Preheat the Ninja Air Fryer to the Air Crisp setting at 180°C (350°F). Using your hands, form small bhajis (fritters) from the onion mixture, pressing them together gently.
3. **Air-crisp the bhajis:** Lightly brush each bhaji with vegetable oil and place them in the air fryer basket in a single layer, ensuring they don't touch. Air-crisp for 10-12 minutes, flipping halfway through, until the bhajis are crispy and golden brown.
4. **Serve:** Serve the onion bhajis hot with a side of chutney or yoghourt dip. These crispy bhajis are perfect as an appetiser or snack.

GRILLED PITA BREAD WITH HUMMUS

Grilled pita bread served with homemade hummus, both made using the Ninja Air Fryer for a healthy, Mediterranean-inspired snack or starter.

Portions: 4 | **Difficulty Level:** Easy | **Preparation Time:** 10 minutes | **Cooking Time**: 10 minutes | **Total Time:** 20 minutes

INGREDIENTS:

- 4 pita breads, halved
- 1 tablespoon olive oil (for brushing)
- 1 can (400 g) chickpeas, drained and rinsed
- 2 tablespoons tahini
- 1 clove garlic, minced
- 1 tablespoon lemon juice
- 1 tablespoon olive oil (for hummus)
- Salt and freshly ground black pepper to taste
- Paprika and fresh parsley (optional, for garnish)

ESTIMATED NUTRITIONAL INFORMATION PER SERVING:
Calories: approx. 250 kcal | Fat: approx. 10 g | Carbohydrates: approx. 30 g | Protein: approx. 7 g | Salt: approx. 0.7 g

INSTRUCTIONS:

1. **Prepare the hummus:** In a food processor, blend the chickpeas, tahini, garlic, lemon juice, and olive oil until smooth. Season with salt and black pepper to taste. If needed, add a tablespoon of water to reach your desired consistency.
2. **Grill the pita bread:** Preheat your Ninja Air Fryer to the Grill setting at 180°C (350°F). Brush the pita halves lightly with olive oil on both sides. Place the pita in the air fryer basket and grill for 3-4 minutes on each side until slightly crispy and golden.
3. **Serve:** Serve the grilled pita bread warm with the hummus on the side. Garnish the hummus with a sprinkle of paprika and fresh parsley for extra flavour.

STUFFED MUSHROOMS WITH GARLIC AND CHEESE

Juicy mushrooms stuffed with garlic and cheese, baked to perfection in the Ninja Air Fryer.

Portions: 4 | **Difficulty Level:** Easy | **Preparation Time:** 10 minutes |
Cooking Time: 10 minutes | **Total Time:** 20 minutes

INGREDIENTS:

- 12 large button mushrooms, stems removed
- 100 g cream cheese
- 50 g cheddar cheese, grated
- 1 clove garlic, minced
- 1 tablespoon fresh parsley, chopped
- 1 tablespoon olive oil
- Salt and freshly ground black pepper to taste

ESTIMATED NUTRITIONAL INFORMATION PER SERVING:
Calories: approx. 150 kcal | Fat: approx. 12 g | Carbohydrates: approx. 4 g |
Protein: approx. 5 g | Salt: approx. 0.6 g

INSTRUCTIONS:

1. **Prepare the filling:** In a small bowl, mix together the cream cheese, grated cheddar, minced garlic, fresh parsley, salt, and pepper until well combined.
2. **Stuff the mushrooms:** Preheat the Ninja Air Fryer to the Bake setting at 180°C (350°F). Brush the mushroom caps with olive oil and stuff each mushroom with a generous amount of the cheese mixture.
3. **Bake the mushrooms:** Place the stuffed mushrooms in the air fryer basket in a single layer. Bake for 8-10 minutes, or until the cheese is melted and the mushrooms are tender.
4. **Serve:** Serve the stuffed mushrooms hot, garnished with extra parsley if desired. These make a great appetiser or snack.

FALAFEL BITES WITH TAHINI SAUCE

Homemade falafel bites, air-crisped until golden, served with a creamy tahini dip.

Portions: 4 | **Difficulty Level:** Medium | **Preparation Time:** 15 minutes | **Cooking Time**: 12 minutes | **Total Time:** 27 minutes

INGREDIENTS:

- 1 can (400 g) chickpeas, drained and rinsed
- 1 small onion, chopped
- 2 cloves garlic, minced
- 2 tablespoons fresh parsley, chopped
- 1 tablespoon flour (or gluten-free alternative)
- 1 teaspoon ground cumin
- 1 teaspoon ground coriander
- 1/2 teaspoon baking powder
- Salt and freshly ground black pepper to taste
- 1 tablespoon olive oil (for brushing)

For the Tahini Sauce:
- 2 tablespoons tahini
- 1 tablespoon lemon juice
- 1 tablespoon water
- Salt and pepper to taste

ESTIMATED NUTRITIONAL INFORMATION PER SERVING:
Calories: approx. 180 kcal | Fat: approx. 8 g | Carbohydrates: approx. 22 g | Protein: approx. 5 g | Salt: approx. 0.7 g

INSTRUCTIONS:

1. **Prepare the falafel mixture:** In a food processor, combine the chickpeas, onion, garlic, parsley, flour, cumin, coriander, baking powder, salt, and pepper. Pulse until the mixture is coarse and sticky, but not fully smooth.
2. **Shape the falafel bites:** Preheat the Ninja Air Fryer to the Air Crisp setting at 200°C (390°F). Using your hands, shape the falafel mixture into small bite-sized balls or patties.
3. **Air-crisp the falafel:** Lightly brush the falafel bites with olive oil and place them in the air fryer basket in a single layer. Air-crisp for 10-12 minutes, flipping halfway through, until golden and crispy.
4. **Make the tahini sauce:** In a small bowl, whisk together the tahini, lemon juice, water, salt, and pepper until smooth and creamy.
5. **Serve:** Serve the falafel bites hot, with the tahini sauce on the side for dipping. These bites are perfect as a snack or as part of a mezze platter.

AIR-FRIED MOZZARELLA STICKS

Crispy on the outside, gooey on the inside, these mozzarella sticks are perfect for dipping.

Portions: 4 | **Difficulty Level:** Medium | **Preparation Time:** 15 minutes (plus 1 hour freezing time) | **Cooking Time**: 8 minutes | **Total Time:** 1 hour 23 minutes

INGREDIENTS:

- 200 g mozzarella cheese, cut into sticks
- 2 large eggs, beaten
- 100 g breadcrumbs
- 50 g plain flour
- 1 teaspoon dried oregano
- 1 teaspoon garlic powder
- Salt and freshly ground black pepper to taste
- Olive oil spray (for crisping)
- Marinara sauce for dipping (optional)

ESTIMATED NUTRITIONAL INFORMATION PER SERVING:
Calories: approx. 220 kcal | Fat: approx. 12 g | Carbohydrates: approx. 15 g | Protein: approx. 10 g | Salt: approx. 0.9 g

INSTRUCTIONS:

1. **Prepare the mozzarella sticks:** Set up a breading station with three bowls: one with flour, one with beaten eggs, and one with breadcrumbs mixed with oregano, garlic powder, salt, and pepper.
2. **Bread the mozzarella sticks:** Coat each mozzarella stick in flour, then dip it into the beaten eggs, and finally coat it in the breadcrumb mixture. For extra crispiness, you can double coat each stick by dipping it again in the egg and breadcrumbs.
3. **Freeze the mozzarella sticks:** Place the breaded mozzarella sticks on a baking sheet lined with parchment paper and freeze for at least 1 hour to prevent the cheese from melting too quickly during cooking.
4. **Air-crisp the mozzarella sticks:** Preheat your Ninja Air Fryer to the Air Crisp setting at 180°C (350°F). Lightly spray the mozzarella sticks with olive oil and place them in the air fryer basket in a single layer. Air-crisp for 6-8 minutes, or until golden and crispy, flipping halfway through.
5. **Serve:** Serve the mozzarella sticks hot with marinara sauce for dipping. These cheesy bites are perfect for a snack or appetiser.

SWEET POTATO FRIES WITH PAPRIKA AND GARLIC

Air-crisped sweet potato fries, seasoned with paprika and garlic for a flavourful and healthy snack.

Portions: 4 | **Difficulty Level:** Easy | **Preparation Time:** 5 minutes | **Cooking Time:** 15 minutes | **Total Time:** 20 minutes

INGREDIENTS:

- 2 medium sweet potatoes, cut into thin fries
- 1 tablespoon olive oil
- 1 teaspoon smoked paprika
- 1/2 teaspoon garlic powder
- Salt and freshly ground black pepper to taste
- Fresh parsley for garnish (optional)

ESTIMATED NUTRITIONAL INFORMATION PER SERVING:
Calories: approx. 180 kcal | Fat: approx. 7 g | Carbohydrates: approx. 25 g | Protein: approx. 2 g | Salt: approx. 0.6 g

INSTRUCTIONS:

1. **Prepare the fries:** Preheat the Ninja Air Fryer to the Air Crisp setting at 200°C (390°F). In a large bowl, toss the sweet potato fries with olive oil, smoked paprika, garlic powder, salt, and black pepper until evenly coated.
2. **Air-crisp the fries:** Place the seasoned sweet potato fries in the air fryer basket in a single layer. Air-crisp for 12-15 minutes, shaking the basket halfway through to ensure even crisping.
3. **Check for doneness:** The fries should be golden and crispy on the outside while tender on the inside. If needed, add an additional 2-3 minutes for extra crispiness.
4. **Serve:** Transfer the crispy sweet potato fries to a serving plate and garnish with fresh parsley if desired. Serve hot as a snack or side dish.

GRILLED CHEESE BITES

Mini grilled cheese sandwiches, air-fried to crispy perfection, ideal as a snack or appetiser.

Portions: 4 | **Difficulty Level:** Easy | **Preparation Time:** 5 minutes |
Cooking Time: 8 minutes | **Total Time:** 13 minutes

INGREDIENTS:

- 8 slices of white or wholemeal bread
- 100 g cheddar cheese, grated
- 2 tablespoons butter, softened
- Salt and freshly ground black pepper to taste
- Tomato ketchup or marinara sauce for dipping (optional)

ESTIMATED NUTRITIONAL INFORMATION PER SERVING:
Calories: approx. 250 kcal | Fat: approx. 15 g | Carbohydrates: approx. 20 g |
Protein: approx. 8 g | Salt: approx. 1.0 g

INSTRUCTIONS:

1. **Assemble the sandwiches:** Preheat the Ninja Air Fryer to the Air Crisp setting at 180°C (350°F). Butter one side of each slice of bread. Place the grated cheddar cheese between two slices of bread, buttered sides facing out, to form mini sandwiches. Season with salt and pepper.
2. **Cut into bites:** Once the sandwiches are assembled, cut them into bite-sized pieces (about 4 squares per sandwich).
3. **Air-crisp the bites:** Place the grilled cheese bites in the air fryer basket in a single layer. Air-crisp for 6-8 minutes, flipping halfway through, until golden and crispy on both sides.
4. **Serve:** Serve the grilled cheese bites hot, with tomato ketchup or marinara sauce for dipping. These cheesy bites are perfect as a snack or appetiser.

STUFFED JALAPEÑOS WITH CREAM CHEESE

Spicy jalapeños stuffed with a creamy cheese filling and air-crisped until golden and bubbly.

Portions: 4 | **Difficulty Level:** Easy | **Preparation Time:** 10 minutes |
Cooking Time: 8 minutes | **Total Time:** 18 minutes

INGREDIENTS:

- 8 large jalapeños, halved and seeds removed
- 150 g cream cheese
- 50 g cheddar cheese, grated
- 1 clove garlic, minced
- 1 tablespoon fresh coriander, chopped
- 1 tablespoon olive oil (for brushing)
- Salt and freshly ground black pepper to taste

ESTIMATED NUTRITIONAL INFORMATION PER SERVING:
Calories: approx. 150 kcal | Fat: approx. 12 g | Carbohydrates: approx. 4 g |
Protein: approx. 5 g | Salt: approx. 0.5 g

INSTRUCTIONS:

1. **Prepare the filling:** In a bowl, mix together the cream cheese, grated cheddar, minced garlic, chopped coriander, salt, and black pepper until well combined.
2. **Stuff the jalapeños:** Preheat the Ninja Air Fryer to the Air Crisp setting at 180°C (350°F). Spoon the cream cheese mixture into each jalapeño half, filling them generously.
3. **Air-crisp the jalapeños:** Lightly brush the tops of the stuffed jalapeños with olive oil and place them in the air fryer basket in a single layer. Air-crisp for 6-8 minutes, or until the tops are golden and the jalapeños are tender.
4. **Serve:** Serve the stuffed jalapeños hot as a snack or appetiser. These spicy bites are perfect for parties or as a side dish.

SPINACH AND RICOTTA PASTRIES

Flaky puff pastries stuffed with a creamy spinach and ricotta filling, air-baked until golden and delicious.

Portions: 4 | **Difficulty Level:** Medium | **Preparation Time:** 15 minutes | **Cooking Time**: 12 minutes | **Total Time:** 27 minutes

INGREDIENTS:

- 1 sheet puff pastry, thawed (ready-made)
- 150 g fresh spinach, wilted and chopped
- 100 g ricotta cheese
- 1 clove garlic, minced
- 1 egg, beaten (for egg wash)
- Salt and freshly ground black pepper to taste
- 1 tablespoon olive oil (for sautéing)

ESTIMATED NUTRITIONAL INFORMATION PER SERVING:
Calories: approx. 250 kcal | Fat: approx. 15 g | Carbohydrates: approx. 20 g | Protein: approx. 8 g | Salt: approx. 0.8 g

INSTRUCTIONS:

1. **Prepare the filling:** Heat the olive oil in a frying-pan over medium heat. Add the minced garlic and sauté for 1-2 minutes until fragrant. Add the spinach and cook until wilted. Remove from heat and allow to cool slightly. Once cooled, mix the spinach with ricotta cheese, salt, and black pepper.
2. **Assemble the pastries:** Preheat the Ninja Air Fryer to the Bake setting at 180°C (350°F). Roll out the puff pastry and cut it into 4 equal squares. Place a spoonful of the spinach and ricotta mixture in the centre of each square. Fold the pastry over the filling to form triangles and press the edges to seal. Brush the tops with beaten egg.
3. **Bake the pastries:** Place the pastries in the air fryer basket and bake for 10-12 minutes, or until golden brown and puffed.
4. **Serve:** Serve the spinach and ricotta pastries hot. They make an excellent appetiser or snack.

CHICKEN AND CHEESE QUESADILLAS

Crispy quesadillas stuffed with seasoned chicken and melted cheese, air-crisped to perfection.

Portions: 4 | **Difficulty Level:** Easy | **Preparation Time:** 10 minutes |
Cooking Time: 8 minutes | **Total Time:** 18 minutes

INGREDIENTS:

- 2 cooked chicken breasts, shredded
- 4 large tortillas
- 150 g cheddar cheese, grated
- 1 tablespoon olive oil
- 1 teaspoon cumin
- 1 teaspoon paprika
- Salt and freshly ground black pepper to taste
- Salsa and sour cream for serving (optional)

ESTIMATED NUTRITIONAL INFORMATION PER SERVING:
Calories: approx. 300 kcal | Fat: approx. 15 g | Carbohydrates: approx. 20 g |
Protein: approx. 20 g | Salt: approx. 1.2 g

INSTRUCTIONS:

1. **Prepare the filling:** In a bowl, mix the shredded chicken with cumin, paprika, salt, and black pepper.
2. **Assemble the quesadillas:** Lay out the tortillas and evenly spread the seasoned chicken and grated cheddar cheese on one half of each tortilla. Fold the tortillas in half to create a half-moon shape.
3. **Air-crisp the quesadillas:** Preheat the Ninja Air Fryer to the Air Crisp setting at 180°C (350°F). Lightly brush the tops of the quesadillas with olive oil and place them in the air fryer basket. Air-crisp for 6-8 minutes, flipping halfway through, until the tortillas are golden and crispy.
4. **Serve:** Cut the quesadillas into wedges and serve hot with salsa and sour cream on the side. These cheesy quesadillas make a quick and satisfying meal or snack.

CHAPTER 3:
MAIN COURSES

WHOLE ROAST CHICKEN WITH LEMON AND THYME

A perfectly roasted chicken, flavoured with lemon and thyme, made using the Roast setting of the Ninja Air Fryer.

Portions: 4-6 | **Difficulty Level:** Medium | **Preparation Time:** 10 minutes | **Cooking Time:** 45-50 minutes | **Total Time:** 55-60 minutes

INGREDIENTS:

- 1 whole chicken (about 1.5 kg)
- 1 lemon, halved
- 3-4 sprigs fresh thyme
- 2 tablespoons olive oil
- 4 cloves garlic, peeled and smashed
- Salt and freshly ground black pepper to taste
- 1 teaspoon paprika (optional)
- 1 onion, quartered (optional)

ESTIMATED NUTRITIONAL INFORMATION PER SERVING:
Calories: approx. 400 kcal | Fat: approx. 25 g | Carbohydrates: approx. 2 g | Protein: approx. 40 g | Salt: approx. 1.2 g

INSTRUCTIONS:

1. **Prepare the chicken:** Preheat your Ninja Air Fryer to the Roast setting at 180°C (350°F). Pat the chicken dry with paper towels. Rub the entire chicken with olive oil and season generously with salt, black pepper, and paprika. Stuff the cavity with the lemon halves, fresh thyme sprigs, and garlic cloves. You can also place the quartered onion inside for extra flavour.

2. **Roast the chicken:** Place the chicken breast-side down in the air fryer basket. Roast for 25 minutes, then flip the chicken breast-side up and continue roasting for another 20-25 minutes, or until the internal temperature reaches 75°C (165°F) and the skin is golden and crispy.

3. **Rest the chicken:** Remove the chicken from the air fryer and let it rest for 10 minutes before carving. This helps the juices redistribute throughout the meat.

4. **Serve:** Carve the chicken and serve with your favourite sides. This roast chicken pairs perfectly with roasted vegetables or a fresh salad.

BEEF WELLINGTON WITH AIR-BAKED PASTRY

A classic beef Wellington with a perfectly crisp pastry shell, made using the Bake function of the Ninja Air Fryer.

Portions: 4 | **Difficulty Level:** Advanced | **Preparation Time:** 25 minutes | **Cooking Time:** 25-30 minutes | **Total Time:** 50-55 minutes

INGREDIENTS:

- 500 g beef fillet
- 1 sheet puff pastry, thawed
- 200 g mushrooms, finely chopped
- 2 tablespoons olive oil
- 1 small onion, finely chopped
- 2 cloves garlic, minced
- 1 tablespoon Dijon mustard
- 4 slices prosciutto
- 1 egg, beaten (for egg wash)
- Salt and freshly ground black pepper to taste

ESTIMATED NUTRITIONAL INFORMATION PER SERVING:
Calories: approx. 600 kcal | Fat: approx. 35 g | Carbohydrates: approx. 30 g | Protein: approx. 40 g | Salt: approx. 1.5 g

INSTRUCTIONS:

1. **Prepare the beef:** Preheat the Ninja Air Fryer to the Bake setting at 180°C (350°F). Season the beef fillet generously with salt and black pepper. Heat 1 tablespoon of olive oil in a frying-pan and sear the beef on all sides until browned (about 2 minutes per side). Remove from heat and set aside.

2. **Prepare the mushroom mixture:** In the same frying-pan, heat the remaining olive oil and sauté the onion, garlic, and mushrooms until the liquid from the mushrooms evaporates and the mixture is dry. Season with salt and pepper. Let it cool.

3. **Assemble the Wellington:** Spread Dijon mustard over the seared beef. Lay the prosciutto slices on a piece of cling film and spread the mushroom mixture on top. Place the beef in the centre and roll it up tightly with the prosciutto and mushrooms.

4. **Wrap in puff pastry:** Roll out the puff pastry and place the beef fillet in the centre. Fold the pastry over the beef, sealing the edges tightly. Brush the pastry with beaten egg and make a few small slits on top for steam to escape.

5. **Bake the Wellington:** Place the wrapped beef Wellington in the air fryer basket and bake for 25-30 minutes, or until the pastry is golden and crisp, and the internal temperature of the beef reaches 54°C (130°F) for medium-rare.

6. **Rest and serve:** Let the Wellington rest for 5 minutes before slicing. Serve with roasted vegetables or mashed potatoes for a classic meal.

FISH AND CHIPS

A healthier version of the traditional British fish and chips, air-crisped to golden perfection.

Portions: 4 | **Difficulty Level:** Medium | **Preparation Time:** 10 minutes |
Cooking Time: 20 minutes | **Total Time:** 30 minutes

INGREDIENTS:

For the Fish:
- 4 fillets of cod (or haddock)
- 50 g plain flour
- 1 large egg, beaten
- 100 g breadcrumbs
- 1 teaspoon paprika
- Salt and freshly ground black pepper to taste

- Olive oil spray

For the Chips:
- 4 large potatoes, cut into thick chips
- 1 tablespoon olive oil
- Salt and freshly ground black pepper to taste
- Malt vinegar for serving (optional)

ESTIMATED NUTRITIONAL INFORMATION PER SERVING:
Calories: approx. 450 kcal | Fat: approx. 15 g | Carbohydrates: approx. 50 g |
Protein: approx. 25 g | Salt: approx. 1.2 g

INSTRUCTIONS:

1. **Prepare the chips:** Preheat the Ninja Air Fryer to the Air Crisp setting at 200°C (390°F). In a large bowl, toss the cut potatoes with olive oil, salt, and black pepper. Place the chips in the air fryer basket in a single layer. Air-crisp for 15-20 minutes, shaking the basket halfway through, until the chips are golden and crispy.

2. **Prepare the fish:** While the chips are cooking, set up a breading station with three bowls: one with flour, one with the beaten egg, and one with breadcrumbs mixed with paprika, salt, and black pepper. Dip each fish fillet first in the flour, then in the egg, and finally in the breadcrumbs, ensuring they are well-coated.

3. **Air-crisp the fish:** Lightly spray the breaded fish fillets with olive oil. Once the chips are done, transfer them to a plate and keep warm. Place the fish fillets in the air fryer basket and air-crisp for 10-12 minutes at 200°C (390°F), flipping halfway through, until golden and cooked through.

4. **Serve:** Serve the crispy fish and chips hot, with a side of malt vinegar and tartar sauce if desired. This healthier version of fish and chips is perfect for a classic British meal.

VEGETARIAN SHEPHERD'S PIE

A hearty plant-based version of the classic shepherd's pie, topped with golden mashed potatoes and air-baked to perfection.

Portions: 4 | **Difficulty Level:** Medium | **Preparation Time:** 15 minutes | **Cooking Time**: 25 minutes | **Total Time:** 40 minutes

INGREDIENTS:

For the Filling:
- 1 tablespoon olive oil
- 1 onion, finely chopped
- 2 cloves garlic, minced
- 2 carrots, diced
- 1 can (400 g) lentils, drained and rinsed
- 1 tablespoon tomato paste
- 200 ml vegetable stock
- 1 teaspoon dried thyme
- 1 teaspoon dried rosemary
- Salt and freshly ground black pepper to taste

For the Mashed Potatoes:
- 4 medium potatoes, peeled and chopped
- 2 tablespoons butter (or plant-based alternative)
- 50 ml milk (or plant-based milk)
- Salt and freshly ground black pepper to taste

ESTIMATED NUTRITIONAL INFORMATION PER SERVING:
Calories: approx. 350 kcal | Fat: approx. 12 g | Carbohydrates: approx. 50 g | Protein: approx. 10 g | Salt: approx. 0.9 g

INSTRUCTIONS:

1. **Prepare the mashed potatoes:** Boil the potatoes in a pot of salted water until tender (about 10-12 minutes). Drain and mash with butter, milk, salt, and black pepper. Set aside.

2. **Prepare the filling:** In a frying-pan, heat the olive oil over medium heat. Add the onion, garlic, and carrots and sauté for 5-7 minutes until softened. Stir in the tomato paste, lentils, thyme, and rosemary. Pour in the vegetable stock and simmer for 5 minutes, until the mixture thickens slightly. Season with salt and pepper to taste.

3. **Assemble the shepherd's pie:** Preheat the Ninja Air Fryer to the Bake setting at 180°C (350°F). Spoon the lentil filling into an air fryer-safe baking dish, then spread the mashed potatoes evenly over the top, using a fork to create texture on the surface.

4. **Bake the shepherd's pie:** Place the baking dish in the air fryer and bake for 15-20 minutes, or until the top is golden and crisp.

5. **Serve:** Let the shepherd's pie cool slightly before serving. This comforting vegetarian dish is perfect for a hearty meal.

LAMB CHOPS WITH ROSEMARY AND GARLIC

Juicy lamb chops infused with the classic flavours of rosemary and garlic, cooked to perfection in the Ninja Air Fryer.

Portions: 4 | **Difficulty Level:** Easy | **Preparation Time:** 10 minutes | **Cooking Time**: 12-15 minutes | **Total Time:** 25 minutes

INGREDIENTS:

- 8 lamb chops (about 2 cm thick)
- 2 tablespoons olive oil
- 3 cloves garlic, minced
- 2 sprigs fresh rosemary, chopped
- Salt and freshly ground black pepper to taste
- Lemon wedges for serving (optional)

ESTIMATED NUTRITIONAL INFORMATION PER SERVING:
Calories: approx. 400 kcal | Fat: approx. 30 g | Carbohydrates: approx. 1 g | Protein: approx. 30 g | Salt: approx. 1.0 g

INSTRUCTIONS:

1. **Prepare the lamb chops:** Preheat the Ninja Air Fryer to the Air Crisp setting at 200°C (390°F). In a small bowl, mix the olive oil, minced garlic, chopped rosemary, salt, and black pepper. Rub this mixture all over the lamb chops, ensuring they are well-coated.
2. **Air-crisp the lamb chops:** Place the lamb chops in the air fryer basket in a single layer. Air-crisp for 12-15 minutes, turning halfway through, until the lamb chops are golden brown and cooked to your desired doneness (internal temperature should reach 60°C for medium).
3. **Rest the lamb chops:** Remove the lamb chops from the air fryer and let them rest for 5 minutes to allow the juices to redistribute.
4. **Serve:** Serve the lamb chops hot, with lemon wedges on the side for a fresh burst of flavour. These tender lamb chops pair beautifully with roasted vegetables or a fresh salad.

GRILLED STEAK WITH CHIMICHURRI

Tender and juicy steaks, grilled to perfection in the Ninja Air Fryer, served with a vibrant chimichurri sauce.

Portions: 4 | **Difficulty Level:** Easy | **Preparation Time:** 15 minutes | **Cooking Time:** 10-12 minutes | **Total Time:** 25-27 minutes

INGREDIENTS:

For the Steak:

- 4 ribeye or sirloin steaks (about 2 cm thick)
- 2 tablespoons olive oil
- Salt and freshly ground black pepper to taste

For the Chimichurri Sauce:

- 1/2 cup fresh parsley, finely chopped
- 1/4 cup fresh coriander, finely chopped
- 2 cloves garlic, minced
- 2 tablespoons red wine vinegar
- 1/2 teaspoon red pepper flakes (optional)
- 1/4 cup olive oil
- Salt and freshly ground black pepper to taste

ESTIMATED NUTRITIONAL INFORMATION PER SERVING:
Calories: approx. 500 kcal | Fat: approx. 35 g | Carbohydrates: approx. 2 g | Protein: approx. 40 g | Salt: approx. 1.2 g

INSTRUCTIONS:

1. **Prepare the chimichurri sauce:** In a small bowl, mix together the parsley, coriander, garlic, red wine vinegar, red pepper flakes (if using), olive oil, salt, and pepper. Stir well and set aside to allow the flavours to meld.
2. **Prepare the steaks:** Preheat the Ninja Air Fryer to the Grill setting at 200°C (390°F). Rub the steaks with olive oil and season generously with salt and black pepper.
3. **Grill the steaks:** Place the steaks in the air fryer basket and grill for 5-6 minutes per side, or until they reach your desired level of doneness (internal temperature should be about 52°C for medium-rare).
4. **Rest the steaks:** Remove the steaks from the air fryer and let them rest for 5 minutes to allow the juices to redistribute.
5. **Serve:** Slice the grilled steaks and serve with a generous spoonful of chimichurri sauce on top. This dish pairs perfectly with roasted vegetables or crispy potato wedges.

STUFFED PEPPERS WITH COUSCOUS AND FETA

Bell peppers stuffed with herbed couscous and feta, air-baked until tender and golden.

Portions: 4 | **Difficulty Level:** Easy | **Preparation Time:** 15 minutes | **Cooking Time:** 15-20 minutes | **Total Time:** 30-35 minutes

INGREDIENTS:

- 4 large bell peppers, halved and seeds removed
- 150 g couscous
- 200 ml vegetable stock
- 100 g feta cheese, crumbled
- 1 small onion, finely chopped
- 1 tablespoon olive oil
- 1 tablespoon fresh parsley, chopped
- 1 teaspoon dried oregano
- Salt and freshly ground black pepper to taste

ESTIMATED NUTRITIONAL INFORMATION PER SERVING:
Calories: approx. 250 kcal | Fat: approx. 12 g | Carbohydrates: approx. 30 g | Protein: approx. 7 g | Salt: approx. 1.0 g

INSTRUCTIONS:

1. **Prepare the couscous:** In a small saucepan, bring the vegetable stock to a boil. Remove from heat, stir in the couscous, cover, and let it sit for 5 minutes until the liquid is absorbed. Fluff the couscous with a fork and set aside.
2. **Prepare the filling:** In a frying-pan, heat the olive oil over medium heat. Add the chopped onion and sauté for 5 minutes until softened. Stir in the cooked couscous, crumbled feta, parsley, oregano, salt, and pepper. Mix well.
3. **Stuff the peppers:** Preheat the Ninja Air Fryer to the Bake setting at 180°C (350°F). Spoon the couscous mixture into each bell pepper half, packing it in tightly.
4. **Bake the stuffed peppers:** Place the stuffed peppers in the air fryer basket in a single layer. Bake for 15-20 minutes, or until the peppers are tender and slightly golden on top.
5. **Serve:** Serve the stuffed peppers hot as a main course or side dish. These peppers pair wonderfully with a fresh salad or yoghourt sauce.

PORK TENDERLOIN WITH APPLES AND ONIONS

Juicy pork tenderloin roasted with sweet apples and caramelised onions, all air-baked to perfection.

Portions: 4 | **Difficulty Level:** Medium | **Preparation Time:** 10 minutes | **Cooking Time**: 20-25 minutes | **Total Time:** 30-35 minutes

INGREDIENTS:

- 500 g pork tenderloin
- 2 apples, cored and sliced
- 1 large onion, sliced
- 2 tablespoons olive oil
- 1 teaspoon dried thyme
- 1 teaspoon Dijon mustard
- Salt and freshly ground black pepper to taste
- 1 tablespoon honey (optional, for a touch of sweetness)

ESTIMATED NUTRITIONAL INFORMATION PER SERVING:
Calories: approx. 350 kcal | Fat: approx. 15 g | Carbohydrates: approx. 20 g | Protein: approx. 30 g | Salt: approx. 1.0 g

INSTRUCTIONS:

1. **Season the pork tenderloin:** Preheat the Ninja Air Fryer to the Roast setting at 180°C (350°F). Rub the pork tenderloin with 1 tablespoon of olive oil, Dijon mustard, thyme, salt, and black pepper.
2. **Prepare the apples and onions:** In a bowl, toss the sliced apples and onions with the remaining olive oil, salt, and pepper. If desired, drizzle with honey for a touch of sweetness.
3. **Roast the pork and vegetables:** Place the pork tenderloin in the air fryer basket, surrounded by the apples and onions. Roast for 20-25 minutes, turning the pork halfway through, until the internal temperature reaches 63°C (145°F) and the apples and onions are caramelised.
4. **Rest the pork:** Remove the pork tenderloin from the air fryer and let it rest for 5 minutes before slicing.
5. **Serve:** Slice the pork tenderloin and serve it with the roasted apples and onions on the side. This dish pairs wonderfully with mashed potatoes or a fresh salad.

VEGETABLE AND CHICKEN SKEWERS

Colourful vegetable and chicken skewers, grilled in the Ninja Air Fryer for a healthy and flavourful meal.

Portions: 4 | **Difficulty Level:** Easy | **Preparation Time:** 15 minutes | **Cooking Time**: 12-15 minutes | **Total Time:** 30 minutes

INGREDIENTS:

- 500 g boneless chicken breasts, cut into cubes
- 1 red bell pepper, cut into chunks
- 1 yellow bell pepper, cut into chunks
- 1 zucchini, sliced into rounds
- 1 red onion, cut into chunks
- 2 tablespoons olive oil
- 2 cloves garlic, minced
- 1 tablespoon lemon juice
- 1 teaspoon dried oregano
- Salt and freshly ground black pepper to taste
- Wooden or metal skewers (soaked if using wooden skewers)

ESTIMATED NUTRITIONAL INFORMATION PER SERVING:
Calories: approx. 300 kcal | Fat: approx. 12 g | Carbohydrates: approx. 10 g | Protein: approx. 35 g | Salt: approx. 1.0 g

INSTRUCTIONS:

1. **Marinate the chicken:** In a large bowl, mix the olive oil, minced garlic, lemon juice, oregano, salt, and black pepper. Add the chicken cubes to the bowl and toss to coat. Let it marinate for 10 minutes while you prepare the vegetables.
2. **Assemble the skewers:** Thread the marinated chicken, bell peppers, zucchini, and red onion onto the skewers, alternating between the chicken and vegetables.
3. **Grill the skewers:** Preheat the Ninja Air Fryer to the Grill setting at 200°C (390°F). Place the skewers in the air fryer basket in a single layer. Grill for 12-15 minutes, turning halfway through, until the chicken is cooked through and the vegetables are slightly charred.
4. **Serve:** Serve the vegetable and chicken skewers hot, with a side of rice or salad. These skewers are perfect for a healthy lunch or dinner.

CRISPY DUCK BREAST WITH ORANGE GLAZE

Air-fried duck breast with a sweet and tangy orange glaze, perfect for an elegant main course.

Portions: 4 | **Difficulty Level:** Medium | **Preparation Time:** 10 minutes |
Cooking Time: 15-18 minutes | **Total Time:** 25-28 minutes

INGREDIENTS:

- 4 duck breasts, skin on
- Salt and freshly ground black pepper to taste
- 1 tablespoon olive oil

For the Orange Glaze:
- 1/2 cup freshly squeezed orange juice
- 1 tablespoon honey
- 1 tablespoon soy sauce
- 1 teaspoon Dijon mustard
- 1 teaspoon orange zest
- 1/2 teaspoon cornflour (for thickening, optional)

ESTIMATED NUTRITIONAL INFORMATION PER SERVING:
Calories: approx. 450 kcal | Fat: approx. 25 g | Carbohydrates: approx. 15 g |
Protein: approx. 35 g | Salt: approx. 1.2 g

INSTRUCTIONS:

1. **Prepare the duck breasts:** Preheat the Ninja Air Fryer to the Air Crisp setting at 200°C (390°F). Score the skin of the duck breasts in a crisscross pattern without cutting into the meat. Rub the duck with olive oil, salt, and black pepper.

2. **Air-crisp the duck breasts:** Place the duck breasts skin-side down in the air fryer basket. Air-crisp for 12-15 minutes, flipping halfway through, until the skin is crispy and the internal temperature reaches 63°C (145°F) for medium doneness. Let the duck rest for 5 minutes before slicing.

3. **Prepare the orange glaze:** While the duck is cooking, combine the orange juice, honey, soy sauce, Dijon mustard, and orange zest in a small saucepan. Bring to a simmer over medium heat. If desired, mix the cornflour with a tablespoon of water to make a slurry, then stir it into the glaze to thicken. Simmer for 2-3 minutes, until slightly reduced.

4. **Serve:** Slice the duck breasts and drizzle the orange glaze over the top. Serve with roasted vegetables or a light salad for an elegant meal.

VEGETARIAN MOUSSAKA

A rich and comforting vegetarian moussaka made with layers of roasted aubergine, spiced lentils, and a creamy béchamel sauce.

Portions: 4 | **Difficulty Level:** Medium | **Preparation Time:** 20 minutes | **Cooking Time:** 30 minutes | **Total Time:** 50 minutes

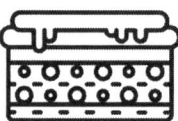

INGREDIENTS:

For the Moussaka:

- 2 large aubergines, sliced into rounds
- 1 can (400 g) lentils, drained and rinsed
- 1 onion, finely chopped
- 2 cloves garlic, minced
- 1 tablespoon olive oil
- 1 tablespoon tomato paste
- 1 teaspoon ground cinnamon
- 1 teaspoon dried oregano
- 400 g chopped tomatoes
- Salt and freshly ground black pepper to taste

For the Béchamel Sauce:

- 2 tablespoons butter (or plant-based alternative)
- 2 tablespoons plain flour
- 300 ml milk (or plant-based milk)
- 1/4 teaspoon ground nutmeg
- 50 g grated cheese (optional, for a richer flavour)

ESTIMATED NUTRITIONAL INFORMATION PER SERVING:
Calories: approx. 350 kcal | Fat: approx. 15 g | Carbohydrates: approx. 40 g | Protein: approx. 12 g | Salt: approx. 1.0 g

INSTRUCTIONS:

1. **Prepare the aubergine:** Preheat the Ninja Air Fryer to the Air Crisp setting at 180°C (350°F). Brush the aubergine slices with olive oil and place them in the air fryer basket in a single layer. Air-crisp for 8-10 minutes, flipping halfway through, until golden and tender. Set aside.

2. **Prepare the lentil filling:** In a frying-pan, heat 1 tablespoon of olive oil over medium heat. Add the onion and garlic and sauté for 5 minutes until softened. Stir in the tomato paste, cinnamon, oregano, lentils, and chopped tomatoes. Simmer for 10 minutes until the mixture thickens. Season with salt and pepper to taste.

3. **Prepare the béchamel sauce:** In a saucepan, melt the butter over medium heat. Stir in the flour and cook for 1-2 minutes until it forms a roux. Gradually whisk in the milk, stirring constantly until the sauce thickens. Add the ground nutmeg and season with salt and pepper. If desired, stir in the grated cheese for a richer béchamel.

4. **Assemble the moussaka:** Preheat the Ninja Air Fryer to the Bake setting at 180°C (350°F). In an air fryer-safe baking dish, layer half of the roasted aubergine slices, followed by the lentil mixture, and then the remaining aubergine slices. Pour the béchamel sauce over the top.

5. **Bake the moussaka:** Place the baking dish in the air fryer and bake for 15-20 minutes, or until the top is golden and bubbling.

6. **Serve:** Allow the moussaka to cool slightly before serving. This vegetarian moussaka is perfect with a fresh salad or crusty bread.

CHICKEN TIKKA WITH SPICY YOGHOURT MARINADE

Tender pieces of chicken marinated in a spiced yoghourt mixture, air-crisped until juicy and served with a cooling yoghourt sauce.

Portions: 4 | **Difficulty Level:** Medium | **Preparation Time:** 15 minutes (plus marinating time) | **Cooking Time:** 15 minutes | **Total Time:** 30 minutes (plus marinating)

INGREDIENTS:

- 500 g boneless chicken thighs, cut into chunks
- 1/2 cup plain yoghourt
- 2 cloves garlic, minced
- 1 tablespoon fresh ginger, grated
- 1 tablespoon lemon juice
- 1 tablespoon olive oil
- 1 teaspoon ground cumin
- 1 teaspoon ground coriander
- 1 teaspoon paprika
- 1/2 teaspoon ground turmeric
- 1/2 teaspoon chili powder (or to taste)
- Salt and freshly ground black pepper to taste

For the Yoghourt Sauce:
- 1/2 cup plain yoghourt
- 1 tablespoon fresh mint, chopped
- 1 tablespoon lemon juice
- Salt and pepper to taste

ESTIMATED NUTRITIONAL INFORMATION PER SERVING:
Calories: approx. 300 kcal | Fat: approx. 15 g | Carbohydrates: approx. 8 g | Protein: approx. 30 g | Salt: approx. 1.0 g

INSTRUCTIONS:

1. **Prepare the marinade:** In a large bowl, combine the yoghourt, garlic, ginger, lemon juice, olive oil, cumin, coriander, paprika, turmeric, chili powder, salt, and black pepper. Mix well.

2. **Marinate the chicken:** Add the chicken chunks to the marinade and toss to coat. Cover and refrigerate for at least 1 hour, or overnight for more flavour.

3. **Air-crisp the chicken:** Preheat the Ninja Air Fryer to the Air Crisp setting at 200°C (390°F). Place the marinated chicken pieces in the air fryer basket in a single layer. Air-crisp for 12-15 minutes, flipping halfway through, until the chicken is golden and cooked through.

4. **Prepare the yoghourt sauce:** While the chicken is cooking, mix together the yoghourt, mint, lemon juice, salt, and pepper in a small bowl.

5. **Serve:** Serve the chicken tikka hot with the cooling yoghourt sauce on the side. This dish pairs perfectly with rice or naan bread.

ROASTED SALMON WITH DILL AND LEMON

Tender salmon fillets, air-baked to perfection with fresh dill and a zesty lemon sauce.

Portions: 4 | **Difficulty Level:** Easy | **Preparation Time:** 5 minutes |
Cooking Time: 10 minutes | **Total Time:** 15 minutes

INGREDIENTS:
- 4 salmon fillets (about 150 g each)
- 1 tablespoon olive oil
- 1 tablespoon fresh dill, chopped
- 1 lemon, sliced into rounds
- 1 tablespoon lemon juice
- Salt and freshly ground black pepper to taste

ESTIMATED NUTRITIONAL INFORMATION PER SERVING:
Calories: approx. 250 kcal | Fat: approx. 15 g | Carbohydrates: approx. 1 g |
Protein: approx. 25 g | Salt: approx. 0.8 g

INSTRUCTIONS:
1. **Prepare the salmon:** Preheat the Ninja Air Fryer to the Bake setting at 180°C (350°F). Brush the salmon fillets with olive oil and season with salt, black pepper, and chopped dill.
2. **Bake the salmon:** Place the salmon fillets skin-side down in the air fryer basket. Arrange the lemon slices on top of each fillet. Bake for 8-10 minutes, or until the salmon is opaque and flakes easily with a fork.
3. **Add lemon juice:** Once the salmon is done, drizzle with fresh lemon juice for an extra zesty kick.
4. **Serve:** Serve the roasted salmon with your favourite sides, such as roasted vegetables or a fresh salad. This light and healthy dish is perfect for a quick and delicious meal.

BEEF AND VEGETABLE STIR-FRY

A quick and easy stir-fry, made with tender beef and crisp vegetables, all cooked to perfection in the Ninja Air Fryer.

Portions: 4 | **Difficulty Level:** Easy | **Preparation Time:** 10 minutes | **Cooking Time:** 12-15 minutes | **Total Time:** 25 minutes

INGREDIENTS:

- 400 g beef sirloin, thinly sliced
- 1 red bell pepper, sliced
- 1 yellow bell pepper, sliced
- 1 courgette, sliced
- 1 carrot, julienned
- 2 tablespoons soy sauce
- 1 tablespoon oyster sauce
- 1 tablespoon sesame oil

- 2 cloves garlic, minced
- 1 tablespoon fresh ginger, grated
- 1 teaspoon cornflour (optional, for thickening sauce)
- Salt and freshly ground black pepper to taste
- Sesame seeds and spring onions for garnish (optional)

ESTIMATED NUTRITIONAL INFORMATION PER SERVING:
Calories: approx. 300 kcal | Fat: approx. 15 g | Carbohydrates: approx. 10 g | Protein: approx. 30 g | Salt: approx. 1.2 g

INSTRUCTIONS:

1. **Marinate the beef:** In a bowl, combine the soy sauce, oyster sauce, sesame oil, garlic, and ginger. Add the sliced beef and toss to coat. Let it marinate for 10 minutes.
2. **Prepare the vegetables:** Preheat the Ninja Air Fryer to the Air Crisp setting at 200°C (390°F). Place the bell peppers, courgette, and carrot in the air fryer basket. Air-crisp for 8-10 minutes, shaking the basket halfway through, until the vegetables are tender and slightly charred.
3. **Cook the beef:** Remove the vegetables from the air fryer and set aside. Place the marinated beef slices in the air fryer basket and air-crisp for 4-5 minutes, or until cooked to your desired doneness.
4. **Combine:** Once the beef is cooked, toss it with the air-fried vegetables. If you prefer a thicker sauce, you can mix the cornflour with a little water and stir it into the stir-fry before serving.
5. **Serve:** Garnish the stir-fry with sesame seeds and chopped spring onions, and serve hot over rice or noodles. This stir-fry is perfect for a quick and healthy dinner.

STUFFED AUBERGINES WITH LENTILS AND FETA

Aubergine halves stuffed with a spiced lentil mixture, air-roasted to perfection and topped with crumbled feta.

Portions: 4 | **Difficulty Level:** Medium | **Preparation Time:** 15 minutes |
Cooking Time: 20 minutes | **Total Time:** 35 minutes

INGREDIENTS:

- 2 large aubergines, halved lengthwise
- 1 tablespoon olive oil
- 1 onion, finely chopped
- 2 cloves garlic, minced
- 1 can (400 g) lentils, drained and rinsed
- 1 teaspoon ground cumin
- 1 teaspoon smoked paprika
- 200 g chopped tomatoes
- 100 g feta cheese, crumbled
- 2 tablespoons fresh parsley, chopped
- Salt and freshly ground black pepper to taste

ESTIMATED NUTRITIONAL INFORMATION PER SERVING:
Calories: approx. 280 kcal | Fat: approx. 10 g | Carbohydrates: approx. 35 g |
Protein: approx. 12 g | Salt: approx. 1.2 g

INSTRUCTIONS:

1. **Prepare the aubergines:** Preheat the Ninja Air Fryer to the Roast setting at 180°C (350°F). Scoop out the flesh from each aubergine half, leaving about 1 cm of flesh inside the skin. Brush the aubergine halves with olive oil, season with salt and pepper, and place them in the air fryer basket. Roast for 12-15 minutes, until tender.
2. **Prepare the filling:** While the aubergines are roasting, heat a frying-pan over medium heat. Add the chopped onion and garlic, and sauté for 5 minutes until softened. Stir in the cumin, smoked paprika, lentils, and chopped tomatoes. Cook for 5 minutes, allowing the mixture to thicken. Season with salt and pepper.
3. **Stuff the aubergines:** Once the aubergines are tender, remove them from the air fryer. Spoon the lentil mixture into each aubergine half, packing it in tightly.
4. **Air-roast the stuffed aubergines:** Place the stuffed aubergines back in the air fryer and roast for an additional 5-7 minutes, until heated through.
5. **Serve:** Top the stuffed aubergines with crumbled feta and chopped parsley before serving. These stuffed aubergines make a perfect vegetarian main course or side dish.

CHAPTER 4: SIDE DISHES

CRISPY SWEET POTATO WEDGES

Air-crisped sweet potato wedges, perfectly seasoned and ideal as a side dish.

Portions: 4 | **Difficulty Level:** Easy | **Preparation Time:** 5 minutes |
Cooking Time: 15 minutes | **Total Time:** 20 minutes

INGREDIENTS:

- 2 large sweet potatoes, cut into wedges
- 1 tablespoon olive oil
- 1 teaspoon smoked paprika
- 1/2 teaspoon garlic powder
- Salt and freshly ground black pepper to taste
- Fresh parsley for garnish (optional)

ESTIMATED NUTRITIONAL INFORMATION PER SERVING:
Calories: approx. 180 kcal | Fat: approx. 6 g | Carbohydrates: approx. 30 g |
Protein: approx. 2 g | Salt: approx. 0.5 g

INSTRUCTIONS:

1. **Prepare the wedges:** Preheat the Ninja Air Fryer to the Air Crisp setting at 200°C (390°F). In a large bowl, toss the sweet potato wedges with olive oil, smoked paprika, garlic powder, salt, and pepper until evenly coated.
2. **Air-crisp the wedges:** Place the sweet potato wedges in the air fryer basket in a single layer. Air-crisp for 12-15 minutes, shaking the basket halfway through, until golden and crispy on the outside, and tender on the inside.
3. **Serve:** Garnish the crispy wedges with fresh parsley and serve hot. These wedges make a great side for any meal or can be enjoyed as a snack.

ROASTED BRUSSELS SPROUTS WITH BACON

Crispy Brussels sprouts paired with savoury bacon, roasted to perfection in the Ninja Air Fryer.

Portions: 4 | **Difficulty Level:** Easy | **Preparation Time:** 5 minutes |
Cooking Time: 12-15 minutes | **Total Time:** 20 minutes

INGREDIENTS:

- 500 g Brussels sprouts, halved
- 4 slices of bacon, chopped
- 1 tablespoon olive oil
- 1 teaspoon garlic powder
- Salt and freshly ground black pepper to taste
- 1 tablespoon balsamic vinegar (optional)

ESTIMATED NUTRITIONAL INFORMATION PER SERVING:
Calories: approx. 200 kcal | Fat: approx. 12 g | Carbohydrates: approx. 15 g |
Protein. approx. 7 g | Salt: approx. 0.8 g

INSTRUCTIONS:

1. **Prepare the Brussels sprouts:** Preheat the Ninja Air Fryer to the Air Crisp setting at 200°C (390°F). In a large bowl, toss the Brussels sprouts with olive oil, garlic powder, salt, and pepper. Add the chopped bacon and toss to combine.

2. **Air-crisp the Brussels sprouts:** Place the Brussels sprouts and bacon mixture in the air fryer basket in a single layer. Air-crisp for 12-15 minutes, shaking the basket halfway through, until the Brussels sprouts are crispy and the bacon is golden.

3. **Serve:** Drizzle the roasted Brussels sprouts with balsamic vinegar for added flavour, if desired. This crispy and savoury side dish pairs perfectly with roasted meats or can be enjoyed on its own.

GRILLED ASPARAGUS WITH LEMON AND PARMESAN

Tender asparagus spears grilled in the Ninja Air Fryer, topped with fresh lemon juice and a sprinkle of Parmesan.

Portions: 4 | **Difficulty Level:** Easy | **Preparation Time:** 5 minutes |
Cooking Time: 8-10 minutes | **Total Time:** 15 minutes

INGREDIENTS:

- 1 bunch of asparagus, trimmed
- 1 tablespoon olive oil
- 1 lemon, zested and juiced
- 2 tablespoons Parmesan cheese, grated
- Salt and freshly ground black pepper to taste

ESTIMATED NUTRITIONAL INFORMATION PER SERVING:
Calories: approx. 100 kcal | Fat: approx. 6 g | Carbohydrates: approx. 5 g |
Protein: approx. 4 g | Salt: approx. 0.5 g

INSTRUCTIONS:

1. **Prepare the asparagus:** Preheat the Ninja Air Fryer to the Grill setting at 200°C (390°F). Toss the asparagus spears with olive oil, salt, and pepper.
2. **Grill the asparagus:** Place the asparagus in the air fryer basket in a single layer. Grill for 8-10 minutes, shaking the basket halfway through, until the asparagus is tender and slightly charred.
3. **Add lemon and Parmesan:** Once the asparagus is done, drizzle with fresh lemon juice and sprinkle with lemon zest and Parmesan cheese.
4. **Serve:** Serve the grilled asparagus hot, with an extra sprinkle of Parmesan if desired. This light and flavourful side dish pairs well with grilled meats or fish.

AIR-CRISPED GREEN BEANS

Green beans air-crisped until tender and golden, a healthy and crispy side dish.

Portions: 4 | **Difficulty Level:** Easy | **Preparation Time:** 5 minutes |
Cooking Time: 10-12 minutes | **Total Time:** 15-17 minutes

INGREDIENTS:

- 400 g green beans, trimmed
- 1 tablespoon olive oil
- 1 teaspoon garlic powder
- Salt and freshly ground black pepper to taste
- 1 tablespoon fresh lemon juice (optional)
- Fresh parsley for garnish (optional)

ESTIMATED NUTRITIONAL INFORMATION PER SERVING:
Calories: approx. 80 kcal | Fat: approx. 5 g | Carbohydrates: approx. 8 g |
Protein: approx. 2 g | Salt: approx. 0.4 g

INSTRUCTIONS:

1. **Prepare the green beans:** Preheat the Ninja Air Fryer to the Air Crisp setting at 200°C (390°F). Toss the green beans with olive oil, garlic powder, salt, and pepper in a large bowl.
2. **Air-crisp the green beans:** Place the green beans in the air fryer basket in a single layer. Air-crisp for 10-12 minutes, shaking the basket halfway through, until the green beans are slightly golden and tender.
3. **Finish with lemon juice:** Once the green beans are done, drizzle with fresh lemon juice for a burst of flavour (optional). Garnish with fresh parsley if desired.
4. **Serve:** Serve the air-crisped green beans hot as a healthy side dish. They pair well with grilled meats, fish, or as a snack.

GARLIC AND HERB ROAST POTATOES

Crispy, golden roast potatoes with a hint of garlic and herbs, made to perfection in the Ninja Air Fryer.

Portions: 4 | **Difficulty Level:** Easy | **Preparation Time:** 5 minutes | **Cooking Time**: 20-25 minutes | **Total Time:** 30 minutes

INGREDIENTS:

- 600 g baby potatoes, halved
- 2 tablespoons olive oil
- 3 cloves garlic, minced
- 1 teaspoon dried rosemary
- 1 teaspoon dried thyme
- Salt and freshly ground black pepper to taste
- Fresh parsley for garnish (optional)

ESTIMATED NUTRITIONAL INFORMATION PER SERVING:
Calories: approx. 180 kcal | Fat: approx. 7 g | Carbohydrates: approx. 30 g | Protein: approx. 3 g | Salt: approx. 0.6 g

INSTRUCTIONS:

1. **Prepare the potatoes:** Preheat the Ninja Air Fryer to the Roast setting at 180°C (350°F). In a large bowl, toss the halved baby potatoes with olive oil, minced garlic, rosemary, thyme, salt, and pepper.
2. **Roast the potatoes:** Place the seasoned potatoes in the air fryer basket in a single layer. Roast for 20-25 minutes, shaking the basket halfway through, until the potatoes are golden and crispy on the outside, and tender on the inside.
3. **Garnish:** Once the potatoes are done, garnish with fresh parsley if desired.
4. **Serve:** Serve the garlic and herb roast potatoes hot as a side dish. They pair perfectly with roasted meats, fish, or even as a snack.

CRISPY CAULIFLOWER BITES

Flavourful cauliflower florets air-crisped to perfection, perfect as a snack or side dish.

Portions: 4 | **Difficulty Level:** Easy | **Preparation Time:** 5 minutes |
Cooking Time: 12-15 minutes | **Total Time:** 20 minutes

INGREDIENTS:

- 1 medium cauliflower, cut into florets
- 2 tablespoons olive oil
- 1 teaspoon smoked paprika
- 1 teaspoon garlic powder
- Salt and freshly ground black pepper to taste
- 2 tablespoons fresh parsley, chopped (for garnish)

ESTIMATED NUTRITIONAL INFORMATION PER SERVING:
Calories: approx. 100 kcal | Fat: approx. 7 g | Carbohydrates: approx. 10 g |
Protein: approx. 3 g | Salt: approx. 0.5 g

INSTRUCTIONS:

1. **Prepare the cauliflower:** Preheat the Ninja Air Fryer to the Air Crisp setting at 200°C (390°F). In a large bowl, toss the cauliflower florets with olive oil, smoked paprika, garlic powder, salt, and pepper until evenly coated.
2. **Air-crisp the cauliflower:** Place the cauliflower florets in the air fryer basket in a single layer. Air-crisp for 12-15 minutes, shaking the basket halfway through, until the cauliflower is golden and crispy on the outside.
3. **Garnish:** Once the cauliflower bites are done, garnish with fresh parsley.
4. **Serve:** Serve the crispy cauliflower bites hot as a side dish or snack. These bites are perfect with a dipping sauce or served alongside grilled meats.

CHEESY CAULIFLOWER BAKE

A creamy and cheesy cauliflower dish, air-baked to golden perfection.

Portions: 4 | **Difficulty Level:** Easy | **Preparation Time:** 10 minutes | **Cooking Time**: 15-20 minutes | **Total Time:** 25-30 minutes

INGREDIENTS:

- 1 medium cauliflower, cut into florets
- 200 ml double cream (or a lighter alternative)
- 100 g cheddar cheese, grated
- 1 teaspoon Dijon mustard
- 1 teaspoon garlic powder
- Salt and freshly ground black pepper to taste
- 2 tablespoons breadcrumbs (optional, for extra crunch)
- Fresh parsley for garnish

ESTIMATED NUTRITIONAL INFORMATION PER SERVING:
Calories: approx. 250 kcal | Fat: approx. 20 g | Carbohydrates: approx. 10 g | Protein: approx. 8 g | Salt: approx. 0.7 g

INSTRUCTIONS:

1. **Prepare the cauliflower:** Preheat the Ninja Air Fryer to the Bake setting at 180°C (350°F). Bring a pot of salted water to a boil and blanch the cauliflower florets for 3-4 minutes until just tender. Drain well.
2. **Prepare the cheese sauce:** In a bowl, mix the double cream, grated cheddar cheese, Dijon mustard, garlic powder, salt, and pepper until well combined.
3. **Assemble the bake:** Transfer the blanched cauliflower florets into an air fryer-safe baking dish. Pour the cheese sauce over the cauliflower, ensuring all florets are coated. If you like extra crunch, sprinkle breadcrumbs over the top.
4. **Bake the cauliflower:** Place the baking dish in the air fryer and bake for 15-20 minutes, until the top is golden and bubbling.
5. **Serve:** Garnish with fresh parsley and serve hot. This cheesy cauliflower bake is the perfect comfort food side dish, great with roasted meats or as a standalone vegetarian meal.

ZUCCHINI FRIES WITH HERB DIP

Crispy zucchini fries, air-crisped to perfection and served with a refreshing herbed yoghourt dip.

Portions: 4 | **Difficulty Level:** Easy | **Preparation Time:** 10 minutes | **Cooking Time:** 10-12 minutes | **Total Time:** 20-22 minutes

INGREDIENTS:

For the Zucchini Fries:
- 2 medium zucchinis, cut into sticks
- 1/2 cup breadcrumbs
- 1/4 cup grated Parmesan cheese
- 1 teaspoon garlic powder
- 1/2 teaspoon paprika
- 2 eggs, beaten
- Salt and freshly ground black pepper to taste

For the Herb Dip:
- 1/2 cup plain yoghourt
- 1 tablespoon fresh parsley, chopped
- 1 tablespoon fresh dill, chopped
- 1 tablespoon lemon juice
- Salt and freshly ground black pepper to taste

ESTIMATED NUTRITIONAL INFORMATION PER SERVING:
Calories: approx. 200 kcal | Fat: approx. 10 g | Carbohydrates: approx. 20 g | Protein: approx. 8 g | Salt: approx. 0.6 g

INSTRUCTIONS:

1. **Prepare the zucchini fries:** Preheat the Ninja Air Fryer to the Air Crisp setting at 200°C (390°F). In a shallow bowl, mix the breadcrumbs, grated Parmesan, garlic powder, paprika, salt, and pepper. Dip each zucchini stick into the beaten eggs, then coat in the breadcrumb mixture.
2. **Air-crisp the zucchini fries:** Place the coated zucchini sticks in the air fryer basket in a single layer. Air-crisp for 10-12 minutes, shaking the basket halfway through, until golden and crispy.
3. **Prepare the herb dip:** In a small bowl, mix the yoghourt, parsley, dill, lemon juice, salt, and pepper until well combined.
4. **Serve:** Serve the zucchini fries hot with the herb dip on the side. These crispy fries are a healthy alternative to regular fries and perfect for snacking or as a side dish.

BAKED POLENTA CHIPS

Crispy baked polenta chips, served with a rich marinara sauce for dipping.

Portions: 4 | **Difficulty Level:** Easy | **Preparation Time:** 10 minutes (plus cooling time) | **Cooking Time:** 15-20 minutes | **Total Time:** 30-35 minutes

INGREDIENTS:

- 250 g instant polenta
- 750 ml vegetable stock
- 50 g Parmesan cheese, grated
- 1 tablespoon olive oil
- Salt and freshly ground black pepper to taste
- 1 teaspoon dried oregano
- Marinara sauce for dipping (optional)

ESTIMATED NUTRITIONAL INFORMATION PER SERVING:
Calories: approx. 200 kcal | Fat: approx. 8 g | Carbohydrates: approx. 30 g | Protein: approx. 6 g | Salt: approx. 0.7 g

INSTRUCTIONS:

1. **Prepare the polenta:** Bring the vegetable stock to a boil in a large pot. Slowly whisk in the polenta, stirring constantly, until thickened (about 5 minutes). Stir in the grated Parmesan, olive oil, salt, pepper, and oregano.
2. **Cool the polenta:** Pour the polenta onto a greased baking sheet and spread it out evenly to about 1 cm thick. Let it cool and firm up for about 30 minutes (or refrigerate for faster cooling).
3. **Cut and bake the polenta chips:** Preheat the Ninja Air Fryer to the Bake setting at 200°C (390°F). Once the polenta has cooled, cut it into chip-shaped sticks. Place the polenta chips in the air fryer basket in a single layer and bake for 15-20 minutes, flipping halfway through, until golden and crispy.
4. **Serve:** Serve the crispy polenta chips with marinara sauce for dipping. These golden chips are a delicious and unique alternative to regular fries.

ROASTED CARROTS WITH HONEY AND THYME

Sweet and tender roasted carrots, glazed with honey and thyme, air-baked to perfection.

Portions: 4 | **Difficulty Level:** Easy | **Preparation Time:** 5 minutes |
Cooking Time: 15-18 minutes | **Total Time:** 20-23 minutes

INGREDIENTS:

- 500 g carrots, peeled and cut into sticks
- 1 tablespoon olive oil
- 1 tablespoon honey
- 1 teaspoon fresh thyme leaves (or 1/2 teaspoon dried thyme)
- Salt and freshly ground black pepper to taste

ESTIMATED NUTRITIONAL INFORMATION PER SERVING:
Calories: approx. 120 kcal | Fat: approx. 5 g | Carbohydrates: approx. 15 g |
Protein: approx. 1 g | Salt: approx. 0.3 g

INSTRUCTIONS:

1. **Prepare the carrots:** Preheat the Ninja Air Fryer to the Roast setting at 180°C (350°F). In a large bowl, toss the carrot sticks with olive oil, honey, thyme, salt, and pepper.
2. **Roast the carrots:** Place the seasoned carrots in the air fryer basket in a single layer. Roast for 15-18 minutes, shaking the basket halfway through, until the carrots are tender and slightly caramelised.
3. **Serve:** Serve the roasted carrots hot, garnished with extra thyme if desired. These sweet and savoury carrots make a perfect side dish for any meal.

MEDITERRANEAN COUSCOUS SALAD

A light and refreshing couscous salad, packed with Mediterranean flavours, perfect as a side dish.

Portions: 4 | **Difficulty Level:** Easy | **Preparation Time:** 10 minutes | **Cooking Time:** 5 minutes | **Total Time:** 15 minutes

INGREDIENTS:

- 150 g couscous
- 200 ml vegetable stock
- 1/2 cucumber, diced
- 100 g cherry tomatoes, halved
- 50 g Kalamata olives, pitted and chopped
- 50 g feta cheese, crumbled
- 2 tablespoons fresh parsley, chopped
- 2 tablespoons olive oil
- 1 tablespoon lemon juice
- Salt and freshly ground black pepper to taste

ESTIMATED NUTRITIONAL INFORMATION PER SERVING:
Calories: approx. 220 kcal | Fat: approx. 10 g | Carbohydrates: approx. 25 g | Protein: approx. 5 g | Salt: approx. 0.8 g

INSTRUCTIONS:

1. **Prepare the couscous:** Bring the vegetable stock to a boil in a small pot. Remove from heat, stir in the couscous, cover, and let it sit for 5 minutes until the liquid is absorbed. Fluff the couscous with a fork and allow it to cool slightly.
2. **Mix the salad:** In a large bowl, combine the diced cucumber, cherry tomatoes, olives, feta cheese, and parsley. Add the cooled couscous and toss gently to combine.
3. **Dress the salad:** Drizzle the olive oil and lemon juice over the salad, then season with salt and pepper. Toss everything together until well mixed.
4. **Serve:** Serve the Mediterranean couscous salad cold or at room temperature. This salad makes a great side dish for grilled meats or can be enjoyed as a light lunch.

GRILLED CORN ON THE COB

Juicy corn cobs grilled in the air fryer, topped with butter and fresh herbs for a burst of flavour.

Portions: 4 | **Difficulty Level:** Easy | **Preparation Time:** 5 minutes |
Cooking Time: 10-12 minutes | **Total Time:** 15-17 minutes

INGREDIENTS:

- 4 ears of corn, husked
- 2 tablespoons butter, melted
- 1 tablespoon fresh parsley, chopped
- Salt and freshly ground black pepper to taste
- Lemon wedges (optional)

ESTIMATED NUTRITIONAL INFORMATION PER SERVING:
Calories: approx. 150 kcal | Fat: approx. 8 g | Carbohydrates: approx. 18 g |
Protein: approx. 3 g | Salt: approx. 0.3 g

INSTRUCTIONS:

1. **Prepare the corn:** Preheat the Ninja Air Fryer to the Grill setting at 200°C (390°F). Brush the corn cobs with melted butter, and season with salt and pepper.
2. **Grill the corn:** Place the corn in the air fryer basket in a single layer. Grill for 10-12 minutes, turning halfway through, until the corn is tender and lightly charred.
3. **Garnish:** Once the corn is done, brush with a little more melted butter and sprinkle with fresh parsley. Squeeze lemon juice over the top for extra flavour if desired.
4. **Serve:** Serve the grilled corn hot, as a delicious side dish or snack. Perfect for barbecues or as a simple summer side.

GARLIC MUSHROOMS

Juicy and savoury garlic mushrooms, roasted to perfection in the air fryer.

Portions: 4 | **Difficulty Level:** Easy | **Preparation Time:** 5 minutes |
Cooking Time: 10-12 minutes | **Total Time:** 15-17 minutes

INGREDIENTS:

- 400 g button mushrooms, cleaned and halved
- 2 tablespoons olive oil
- 3 cloves garlic, minced
- 1 tablespoon fresh parsley, chopped
- 1 teaspoon dried thyme
- Salt and freshly ground black pepper to taste
- Lemon wedges (optional)

ESTIMATED NUTRITIONAL INFORMATION PER SERVING:
Calories: approx. 120 kcal | Fat: approx. 8 g | Carbohydrates: approx. 5 g |
Protein: approx. 3 g | Salt: approx. 0.4 g

INSTRUCTIONS:

1. **Prepare the mushrooms:** Preheat the Ninja Air Fryer to the Air Crisp setting at 200°C (390°F). In a large bowl, toss the mushrooms with olive oil, minced garlic, thyme, salt, and pepper until evenly coated.
2. **Air-crisp the mushrooms:** Place the mushrooms in the air fryer basket in a single layer. Air-crisp for 10-12 minutes, shaking the basket halfway through, until the mushrooms are golden and tender.
3. **Garnish:** Once the mushrooms are done, sprinkle with fresh parsley and squeeze lemon juice over the top if desired.
4. **Serve:** Serve the garlic mushrooms hot as a side dish or appetiser. These mushrooms pair perfectly with grilled meats or as a topping for toast.

ROASTED BELL PEPPERS

Colourful bell peppers roasted with olive oil and herbs, a versatile and flavourful side dish.

Portions: 4 | **Difficulty Level:** Easy | **Preparation Time:** 5 minutes |
Cooking Time: 12-15 minutes | **Total Time:** 20 minutes

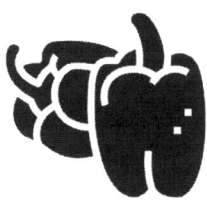

INGREDIENTS:
- 3 bell peppers (red, yellow, and orange), sliced into strips
- 1 tablespoon olive oil
- 1 teaspoon dried oregano
- 1/2 teaspoon garlic powder
- Salt and freshly ground black pepper to taste
- Fresh basil leaves for garnish (optional)

ESTIMATED NUTRITIONAL INFORMATION PER SERVING:
Calories: approx. 90 kcal | Fat: approx. 5 g | Carbohydrates: approx. 10 g |
Protein: approx. 1 g | Salt: approx. 0.3 g

INSTRUCTIONS:
1. **Prepare the bell peppers:** Preheat the Ninja Air Fryer to the Air Crisp setting at 200°C (390°F). In a large bowl, toss the bell pepper strips with olive oil, oregano, garlic powder, salt, and pepper until evenly coated.
2. **Air-crisp the bell peppers:** Place the peppers in the air fryer basket in a single layer. Air-crisp for 12-15 minutes, shaking the basket halfway through, until the peppers are soft and slightly charred.
3. **Garnish:** Once the peppers are done, garnish with fresh basil leaves if desired.
4. **Serve:** Serve the roasted bell peppers hot as a side dish or use them as a topping for salads, sandwiches, or pasta. These peppers are perfect for adding a burst of colour and flavour to any meal.

CRISPY ONION RINGS

Crispy, golden onion rings, air-crisped to perfection for a delicious snack or side dish.

Portions: 4 | **Difficulty Level:** Easy | **Preparation Time:** 10 minutes |
Cooking Time: 10-12 minutes | **Total Time:** 20-22 minutes

INGREDIENTS:

- 2 large onions, sliced into rings
- 1/2 cup all-purpose flour
- 1/2 cup breadcrumbs
- 1/4 cup grated Parmesan cheese (optional)
- 1 teaspoon paprika
- 1 teaspoon garlic powder
- 2 eggs, beaten
- Salt and freshly ground black pepper to taste

ESTIMATED NUTRITIONAL INFORMATION PER SERVING:
Calories: approx. 200 kcal | Fat: approx. 8 g | Carbohydrates: approx. 25 g |
Protein: approx. 6 g | Salt: approx. 0.5 g

INSTRUCTIONS:

1. **Prepare the coating:** Preheat the Ninja Air Fryer to the Air Crisp setting at 200°C (390°F). In one bowl, mix the flour, paprika, garlic powder, salt, and pepper. In a second bowl, beat the eggs. In a third bowl, mix the breadcrumbs and Parmesan cheese (if using).
2. **Coat the onion rings:** Dip each onion ring into the flour mixture, then into the beaten eggs, and finally coat with the breadcrumb mixture.
3. **Air-crisp the onion rings:** Place the coated onion rings in the air fryer basket in a single layer. Air-crisp for 10-12 minutes, flipping halfway through, until golden and crispy.
4. **Serve:** Serve the crispy onion rings hot, with your favourite dipping sauce. These onion rings are a perfect side dish or snack, crispy on the outside and tender on the inside.

CHAPTER 5: DESSERTS

AIR-FRIED APPLE CRUMBLE

A classic apple crumble made with tender apples and a buttery oat topping, baked to perfection in the Ninja Air Fryer.

Portions: 4 | **Difficulty Level:** Easy | **Preparation Time:** 10 minutes | **Cooking Time**: 15-18 minutes | **Total Time:** 25-28 minutes

INGREDIENTS:

- 4 medium apples, peeled, cored, and sliced
- 2 tablespoons brown sugar
- 1 teaspoon ground cinnamon
- 1 tablespoon lemon juice

For the Crumble Topping:

- 75 g rolled oats
- 50 g plain flour
- 50 g butter, cold and cut into small pieces
- 50 g brown sugar
- 1/2 teaspoon ground cinnamon

ESTIMATED NUTRITIONAL INFORMATION PER SERVING:
Calories: approx. 250 kcal | Fat: approx. 10 g | Carbohydrates: approx. 40 g | Protein: approx. 3 g | Salt: approx. 0.2 g

INSTRUCTIONS:

1. **Prepare the apples:** Preheat the Ninja Air Fryer to the Bake setting at 180°C (350°F). In a bowl, toss the sliced apples with brown sugar, cinnamon, and lemon juice. Place the apple mixture in an air fryer-safe baking dish.
2. **Prepare the crumble topping:** In another bowl, mix the oats, flour, brown sugar, and cinnamon. Add the cold butter and use your fingertips to rub the butter into the dry ingredients until the mixture resembles coarse crumbs.
3. **Assemble and bake:** Sprinkle the crumble topping evenly over the apples. Place the baking dish in the air fryer and bake for 15-18 minutes, until the topping is golden and the apples are tender.
4. **Serve:** Serve the apple crumble warm, optionally with a scoop of vanilla ice cream or a dollop of cream. This comforting dessert is perfect for any time of year.

STICKY TOFFEE PUDDING

A rich and moist British dessert, filled with dates and topped with a sweet, sticky toffee sauce, baked in the Ninja Air Fryer.

Portions: 4 | **Difficulty Level:** Medium | **Preparation Time:** 15 minutes | **Cooking Time:** 20-25 minutes | **Total Time:** 40 minutes

INGREDIENTS:

For the Pudding:
- 175 g dates, pitted and chopped
- 200 ml boiling water
- 1 teaspoon bicarbonate of soda
- 75 g unsalted butter, softened
- 150 g dark brown sugar
- 2 large eggs
- 175 g self-raising flour
- 1 teaspoon vanilla extract

For the Toffee Sauce:
- 100 g unsalted butter
- 150 g dark brown sugar
- 200 ml double cream
- 1 teaspoon vanilla extract

ESTIMATED NUTRITIONAL INFORMATION PER SERVING:
Calories: approx. 500 kcal | Fat: approx. 25 g | Carbohydrates: approx. 65 g | Protein: approx. 6 g | Salt: approx. 0.3 g

INSTRUCTIONS:

1. **Prepare the dates:** Place the chopped dates in a bowl and pour over the boiling water. Stir in the bicarbonate of soda and let it sit for 10 minutes, until the dates soften.
2. **Make the pudding batter:** Preheat the Ninja Air Fryer to the Bake setting at 160°C (320°F). In a large mixing bowl, cream together the softened butter and dark brown sugar until light and fluffy. Beat in the eggs one at a time, then stir in the vanilla extract. Gradually fold in the self-raising flour and the softened dates (with the soaking liquid) until well combined.
3. **Bake the pudding:** Transfer the batter to an air fryer-safe baking dish and smooth the top. Bake in the air fryer for 20-25 minutes, until the pudding is golden and firm to the touch.
4. **Make the toffee sauce:** While the pudding is baking, prepare the toffee sauce. In a saucepan, melt the butter over medium heat. Stir in the dark brown sugar and double cream, then bring to a gentle simmer. Cook for 3-4 minutes, stirring frequently, until the sauce thickens. Remove from heat and stir in the vanilla extract.
5. **Serve:** Once the pudding is done, pour some of the warm toffee sauce over the top and let it soak in. Serve with extra sauce on the side.

CRISPY CHURROS WITH CHOCOLATE DIP

Light and crispy churros, coated in cinnamon sugar and served with a rich chocolate dipping sauce.

Portions: 4 | **Difficulty Level:** Medium | **Preparation Time:** 10 minutes | **Cooking Time**: 10 minutes | **Total Time:** 20 minutes

INGREDIENTS:

- **For the Churros:**
- 125 g plain flour
- 1 tablespoon sugar
- 1/2 teaspoon baking powder
- 1/4 teaspoon salt
- 1 tablespoon butter

- 250 ml water
- 1 teaspoon vanilla extract
- 1 egg, lightly beaten
- 50 g sugar (for coating)
- 1 teaspoon ground cinnamon (for coating)

For the Chocolate Dip:
- 100 g dark chocolate, chopped
- 100 ml double cream
- 1 tablespoon sugar

ESTIMATED NUTRITIONAL INFORMATION PER SERVING:
Calories: approx. 350 kcal | Fat: approx. 20 g | Carbohydrates: approx. 45 g | Protein: approx. 5 g | Salt: approx. 0.4 g

INSTRUCTIONS:

1. **Prepare the dough:** In a saucepan, combine the water, butter, and 1 tablespoon of sugar. Bring to a boil, then remove from heat. Stir in the flour, baking powder, and salt until the mixture forms a smooth dough. Let the dough cool slightly, then mix in the vanilla extract and beaten egg until well combined.
2. **Shape the churros:** Preheat the Ninja Air Fryer to the Air Crisp setting at 200°C (390°F). Transfer the dough to a piping bag fitted with a star tip. Pipe the dough into churro shapes (about 10 cm long) onto a piece of parchment paper.
3. **Air-crisp the churros:** Place the churros in the air fryer basket in a single layer. Air-crisp for 8-10 minutes, or until golden and crispy.
4. **Coat the churros:** In a shallow bowl, mix together the 50 g sugar and cinnamon. Roll the hot churros in the cinnamon sugar mixture to coat.
5. **Make the chocolate dip:** In a small saucepan, heat the double cream until it begins to simmer. Remove from heat and stir in the chopped dark chocolate and sugar until smooth.
6. **Serve:** Serve the crispy churros hot, with the chocolate dip on the side.

MINI VICTORIA SPONGE CAKES

Delicate mini Victoria sponge cakes filled with jam and whipped cream, baked to perfection in the Ninja Air Fryer.

Portions: 4 | **Difficulty Level:** Medium | **Preparation Time:** 15 minutes | **Cooking Time:** 12-15 minutes | **Total Time:** 30 minutes

INGREDIENTS:

For the Sponge Cakes:
- 100 g self-raising flour
- 100 g unsalted butter, softened
- 100 g caster sugar
- 2 large eggs
- 1 teaspoon vanilla extract

- 1 tablespoon milk (if needed)

For the Filling:
- 100 ml double cream
- 2 tablespoons strawberry or raspberry jam
- Icing sugar for dusting

ESTIMATED NUTRITIONAL INFORMATION PER SERVING:
Calories: approx. 300 kcal | Fat: approx. 20 g | Carbohydrates: approx. 30 g | Protein: approx. 4 g | Salt: approx. 0.3 g

INSTRUCTIONS:

1. **Prepare the sponge batter:** Preheat the Ninja Air Fryer to the Bake setting at 160°C (320°F). In a large bowl, cream together the softened butter and caster sugar until light and fluffy. Add the eggs one at a time, beating well after each addition. Stir in the vanilla extract. Gently fold in the self-raising flour, adding a little milk if needed to achieve a smooth batter.

2. **Bake the mini cakes:** Divide the batter between greased mini cake moulds or cupcake cases. Place the moulds in the air fryer basket and bake for 12-15 minutes, or until the cakes are golden and a skewer inserted into the centre comes out clean. Allow the cakes to cool completely.

3. **Prepare the filling:** While the cakes are cooling, whip the double cream until soft peaks form.

4. **Assemble the cakes:** Once the cakes are cool, slice them in half horizontally. Spread a layer of jam on the bottom half of each cake, then spoon or pipe the whipped cream on top. Place the top half of the cake back on and dust with icing sugar.

5. **Serve:** Serve the mini Victoria sponge cakes with a light dusting of icing sugar. These classic cakes are perfect for an afternoon tea or a sweet treat.

BERRY CRUMBLE WITH OATS

A warm and fruity berry crumble with a crunchy oat topping, baked to perfection in the Ninja Air Fryer.

Portions: 4 | **Difficulty Level:** Easy | **Preparation Time:** 10 minutes | **Cooking Time**: 15-18 minutes | **Total Time:** 25-28 minutes

INGREDIENTS:

For the Filling:
- 300 g mixed berries (such as strawberries, blueberries, and raspberries)
- 2 tablespoons sugar
- 1 tablespoon lemon juice
- 1 teaspoon vanilla extract

For the Crumble Topping:
- 75 g rolled oats
- 50 g plain flour
- 50 g butter, cold and cut into small cubes
- 50 g brown sugar
- 1/2 teaspoon ground cinnamon

ESTIMATED NUTRITIONAL INFORMATION PER SERVING:
Calories: approx. 240 kcal | Fat: approx. 10 g | Carbohydrates: approx. 35 g | Protein: approx. 3 g | Salt: approx. 0.2 g

INSTRUCTIONS:

1. **Prepare the berry filling:** Preheat the Ninja Air Fryer to the Bake setting at 180°C (350°F). In a bowl, toss the mixed berries with sugar, lemon juice, and vanilla extract. Transfer the berry mixture to an air fryer-safe baking dish.
2. **Prepare the crumble topping:** In a separate bowl, mix together the oats, flour, brown sugar, and cinnamon. Add the cold butter and use your fingertips to rub the butter into the dry ingredients until the mixture resembles coarse crumbs.
3. **Assemble and bake:** Sprinkle the crumble topping evenly over the berry mixture. Place the baking dish in the air fryer and bake for 15-18 minutes, until the topping is golden and the berries are bubbling.
4. **Serve:** Serve the berry crumble warm, optionally with a scoop of vanilla ice cream or a dollop of whipped cream. This fruity crumble is perfect for a comforting dessert.

BANANA BREAD

A moist and fluffy banana bread, made with ripe bananas and baked to perfection in the Ninja Air Fryer.

Portions: 8 slices | **Difficulty Level:** Easy | **Preparation Time:** 10 minutes | **Cooking Time**: 25-30 minutes | **Total Time:** 40 minutes

INGREDIENTS:

- 2 ripe bananas, mashed
- 100 g unsalted butter, softened
- 100 g caster sugar
- 2 large eggs
- 150 g self-raising flour
- 1 teaspoon baking powder
- 1 teaspoon vanilla extract
- 1/4 teaspoon ground cinnamon (optional)
- 50 g chopped walnuts or chocolate chips (optional)

ESTIMATED NUTRITIONAL INFORMATION PER SLICE:
Calories: approx. 200 kcal | Fat: approx. 10 g | Carbohydrates: approx. 25 g | Protein: approx. 3 g | Salt: approx. 0.3 g

INSTRUCTIONS:

1. **Prepare the batter:** Preheat the Ninja Air Fryer to the Bake setting at 160°C (320°F). In a large mixing bowl, cream together the softened butter and caster sugar until light and fluffy. Beat in the eggs one at a time, then stir in the vanilla extract and mashed bananas.

2. **Add the dry ingredients:** In a separate bowl, sift together the self-raising flour, baking powder, and cinnamon (if using). Gently fold the dry ingredients into the wet mixture until just combined. If using, fold in the chopped walnuts or chocolate chips.

3. **Bake the banana bread:** Grease an air fryer-safe loaf pan and pour in the batter. Smooth the top and place the loaf pan in the air fryer basket. Bake for 25-30 minutes, or until a skewer inserted into the centre comes out clean. If the top browns too quickly, cover loosely with foil halfway through.

4. **Cool and serve:** Allow the banana bread to cool in the pan for 10 minutes before transferring to a wire rack to cool completely. Serve in slices with butter or enjoy on its own as a sweet snack.

CHOCOLATE CHIP COOKIES

Soft and chewy cookies with crispy edges, filled with gooey chocolate chips, air-baked to perfection.

Portions: 12 cookies | **Difficulty Level:** Easy | **Preparation Time:** 10 minutes | **Cooking Time**: 8-10 minutes | **Total Time:** 20 minutes

INGREDIENTS:

- 100 g unsalted butter, softened
- 100 g caster sugar
- 50 g light brown sugar
- 1 large egg

- 1 teaspoon vanilla extract
- 150 g self-raising flour
- 100 g chocolate chips (milk, dark, or a mix)
- Pinch of salt

ESTIMATED NUTRITIONAL INFORMATION PER COOKIE:
Calories: approx. 150 kcal | Fat: approx. 7 g | Carbohydrates: approx. 20 g | Protein: approx. 2 g | Salt: approx. 0.2 g

INSTRUCTIONS:

1. **Prepare the cookie dough:** Preheat the Ninja Air Fryer to the Bake setting at 160°C (320°F). In a large mixing bowl, cream together the softened butter, caster sugar, and light brown sugar until light and fluffy. Beat in the egg and vanilla extract until well combined.
2. **Add the dry ingredients:** Sift in the self-raising flour and add a pinch of salt. Mix until just combined, then fold in the chocolate chips.
3. **Shape the cookies:** Scoop tablespoon-sized portions of the dough and roll them into balls. Place the cookie dough balls on a baking sheet lined with parchment paper, leaving space between them for spreading.
4. **Bake the cookies:** Place the baking sheet in the air fryer basket and bake for 8-10 minutes, or until the cookies are golden around the edges and slightly soft in the centre. Let the cookies cool on the baking sheet for 5 minutes before transferring to a wire rack to cool completely.
5. **Serve:** Serve the cookies warm or at room temperature. These chocolate chip cookies are perfect for dunking in milk or enjoying on their own.

CINNAMON ROLLS WITH ICING

Warm, gooey cinnamon rolls baked in the Ninja Air Fryer, topped with sweet icing for a delicious treat.

Portions: 6 rolls | **Difficulty Level:** Medium | **Preparation Time:** 15 minutes (plus rising time) | **Cooking Time:** 12-15 minutes | **Total Time:** 1 hour 30 minutes (including rising time)

INGREDIENTS:

For the Dough:
- 150 ml warm milk
- 50 g unsalted butter, melted
- 1 large egg
- 250 g strong white bread flour
- 25 g caster sugar
- 7 g (1 packet) instant yeast
- Pinch of salt

For the Filling:
- 50 g unsalted butter, softened
- 75 g brown sugar
- 1 tablespoon ground cinnamon

For the Icing:
- 100 g icing sugar
- 2 tablespoons milk
- 1/2 teaspoon vanilla extract

ESTIMATED NUTRITIONAL INFORMATION PER ROLL:
Calories: approx. 300 kcal | Fat: approx. 12 g | Carbohydrates: approx. 40 g | Protein: approx. 5 g | Salt: approx. 0.3 g

INSTRUCTIONS:

1. **Prepare the dough:** In a mixing bowl, combine the warm milk, melted butter, and egg. In a separate bowl, mix the flour, caster sugar, yeast, and salt. Gradually add the wet ingredients to the dry ingredients, mixing until a dough forms. Knead the dough for 5-7 minutes, until smooth and elastic. Place the dough in a lightly greased bowl, cover, and let rise in a warm place for about 1 hour, or until doubled in size.

2. **Prepare the filling:** In a small bowl, mix the softened butter, brown sugar, and cinnamon until well combined.

3. **Assemble the rolls:** Once the dough has risen, roll it out on a lightly floured surface into a rectangle about 1 cm thick. Spread the cinnamon filling evenly over the dough. Roll the dough up tightly from the long side, then cut into 6 equal slices.

4. **Bake the cinnamon rolls:** Preheat the Ninja Air Fryer to the Bake setting at 160°C (320°F). Place the cinnamon rolls in an air fryer-safe baking dish, leaving space between them to rise. Bake for 12-15 minutes, or until golden and cooked through.

5. **Make the icing:** While the rolls are baking, whisk together the icing sugar, milk, and vanilla extract until smooth.

6. **Serve:** Drizzle the warm cinnamon rolls with the icing and serve immediately. These cinnamon rolls are best enjoyed warm and gooey, perfect for a sweet breakfast or snack.

LEMON DRIZZLE CAKE

A zesty and moist lemon cake with a sweet drizzle, air-baked to perfection in the Ninja Air Fryer.

Portions: 8 slices | **Difficulty Level:** Easy | **Preparation Time:** 10 minutes | **Cooking Time:** 25-30 minutes | **Total Time:** 40 minutes

INGREDIENTS:

For the Cake:
- 150 g self-raising flour
- 150 g unsalted butter, softened
- 150 g caster sugar
- 2 large eggs
- Zest of 2 lemons

- 2 tablespoons lemon juice
- 1 teaspoon vanilla extract

For the Drizzle:
- 50 g icing sugar
- Juice of 1 lemon

ESTIMATED NUTRITIONAL INFORMATION PER SLICE:
Calories: approx. 230 kcal | Fat: approx. 12 g | Carbohydrates: approx. 30 g | Protein: approx. 3 g | Salt: approx. 0.3 g

INSTRUCTIONS:

1. **Prepare the batter:** Preheat the Ninja Air Fryer to the Bake setting at 160°C (320°F). In a large mixing bowl, cream together the softened butter and caster sugar until light and fluffy. Beat in the eggs, one at a time, then stir in the lemon zest, lemon juice, and vanilla extract.

2. **Add the dry ingredients:** Gently fold the self-raising flour into the wet mixture until just combined, being careful not to overmix.

3. **Bake the cake:** Grease an air fryer-safe loaf pan and pour the batter in. Smooth the top and place the loaf pan in the air fryer basket. Bake for 25-30 minutes, or until a skewer inserted into the centre comes out clean. If the top browns too quickly, cover loosely with foil halfway through.

4. **Make the drizzle:** While the cake is baking, mix the icing sugar and lemon juice until smooth. Once the cake is out of the air fryer, poke holes all over the top with a skewer and pour the lemon drizzle over the warm cake.

5. **Serve:** Allow the lemon drizzle cake to cool before slicing. This zesty cake is perfect for an afternoon treat or dessert.

BAKED APPLES WITH CINNAMON

Warm and tender apples filled with a cinnamon and sugar mixture, baked to perfection in the Ninja Air Fryer.

Portions: 4 | **Difficulty Level:** Easy | **Preparation Time:** 10 minutes | **Cooking Time**: 15-18 minutes | **Total Time:** 25-28 minutes

INGREDIENTS:

- 4 medium apples (such as Braeburn or Granny Smith)
- 2 tablespoons brown sugar
- 1 teaspoon ground cinnamon
- 1 tablespoon butter, cut into small cubes
- 2 tablespoons chopped walnuts or pecans (optional)
- Vanilla ice cream or whipped cream for serving (optional)

ESTIMATED NUTRITIONAL INFORMATION PER SERVING:
Calories: approx. 150 kcal (without ice cream) | Fat: approx. 5 g | Carbohydrates: approx. 25 g | Protein: approx. 1 g | Salt: approx. 0.1 g

INSTRUCTIONS:

1. **Prepare the apples:** Preheat the Ninja Air Fryer to the Bake setting at 180°C (350°F). Core the apples, leaving the bottom intact, and create a hollow space for the filling.
2. **Make the filling:** In a small bowl, mix the brown sugar, cinnamon, and chopped nuts (if using). Stuff each apple with the sugar mixture and top with a small cube of butter.
3. **Bake the apples:** Place the stuffed apples in an air fryer-safe dish and bake in the air fryer for 15-18 minutes, or until the apples are tender and the filling is bubbling.
4. **Serve:** Serve the baked apples warm, optionally with a scoop of vanilla ice cream or a dollop of whipped cream. These baked apples are a comforting and delicious dessert for any occasion.

PEACH COBBLER

A classic British peach cobbler, baked with a golden biscuit topping in the Ninja Air Fryer.

Portions: 4 | **Difficulty Level:** Easy | **Preparation Time:** 10 minutes |
Cooking Time: 15-18 minutes | **Total Time:** 25-28 minutes

INGREDIENTS:

For the Filling:
- 400 g canned peaches (in juice), drained and sliced
- 2 tablespoons brown sugar
- 1 teaspoon vanilla extract
- 1/2 teaspoon ground cinnamon

For the Biscuit Topping:
- 100 g self-raising flour
- 50 g unsalted butter, cold and cut into small cubes
- 2 tablespoons caster sugar
- 50 ml milk

ESTIMATED NUTRITIONAL INFORMATION PER SERVING:
Calories: approx. 250 kcal | Fat: approx. 10 g | Carbohydrates: approx. 35 g |
Protein: approx. 3 g | Salt: approx. 0.2 g

INSTRUCTIONS:

1. **Prepare the peach filling:** Preheat the Ninja Air Fryer to the Bake setting at 180°C (350°F). In a bowl, toss the sliced peaches with brown sugar, vanilla extract, and cinnamon. Transfer the peach mixture to an air fryer-safe baking dish.
2. **Make the biscuit topping:** In a separate bowl, rub the cold butter into the self-raising flour until the mixture resembles coarse crumbs. Stir in the sugar, then add the milk gradually, stirring until a soft dough forms.
3. **Assemble the cobbler:** Drop spoonfuls of the biscuit dough on top of the peaches, leaving some gaps for the cobbler to bubble through.
4. **Bake the cobbler:** Place the baking dish in the air fryer and bake for 15-18 minutes, or until the topping is golden and the filling is bubbly.
5. **Serve:** Serve the peach cobbler warm, optionally with a scoop of vanilla ice cream or a dollop of cream. This cobbler is the perfect blend of sweet peaches and buttery biscuit topping.

CHOCOLATE LAVA CAKES

Rich, molten-centred chocolate cakes, air-baked for a decadent and indulgent dessert.

Portions: 4 | **Difficulty Level:** Medium | **Preparation Time:** 10 minutes | **Cooking Time**: 8-10 minutes | **Total Time:** 20 minutes

INGREDIENTS:

- 100 g dark chocolate, chopped
- 75 g unsalted butter
- 50 g caster sugar
- 2 large eggs
- 1 teaspoon vanilla extract
- 40 g plain flour
- Pinch of salt
- Cocoa powder (for dusting)

ESTIMATED NUTRITIONAL INFORMATION PER SERVING:
Calories: approx. 300 kcal | Fat: approx. 20 g | Carbohydrates: approx. 25 g | Protein: approx. 5 g | Salt: approx. 0.2 g

INSTRUCTIONS:

1. **Melt the chocolate:** Preheat the Ninja Air Fryer to the Bake setting at 180°C (350°F). In a heatproof bowl, melt the dark chocolate and butter together over a pan of simmering water, stirring until smooth. Remove from heat and allow to cool slightly.
2. **Prepare the batter:** In a separate bowl, whisk together the eggs, caster sugar, and vanilla extract until light and fluffy. Gently fold the melted chocolate into the egg mixture. Sift in the plain flour and salt, and fold until just combined.
3. **Prepare the ramekins:** Grease 4 small ramekins with butter and dust the insides with cocoa powder. Divide the batter evenly between the ramekins.
4. **Bake the lava cakes:** Place the ramekins in the air fryer basket and bake for 8-10 minutes, or until the edges are set but the centres are still soft.
5. **Serve:** Allow the cakes to cool for 1-2 minutes before carefully turning them out onto plates. Serve the lava cakes warm, with a dusting of icing sugar or a scoop of vanilla ice cream. These lava cakes have a rich, gooey centre that makes for an unforgettable dessert.

AIR-FRIED DONUTS

Light and fluffy donuts with a crispy exterior, coated in sugar or glazed, made using the Ninja Air Fryer.

Portions: 8 donuts | **Difficulty Level:** Medium | **Preparation Time:** 15 minutes (plus rising time) | **Cooking Time**: 8-10 minutes | **Total Time:** 1 hour 30 minutes (including rising time)

INGREDIENTS:

For the Donuts:
- 200 g strong white bread flour
- 25 g caster sugar
- 7 g (1 packet) instant yeast
- 1 large egg
- 50 ml warm milk
- 30 g unsalted butter, melted
- Pinch of salt

For Coating:
- 50 g sugar
- 1 teaspoon ground cinnamon (optional)
- Melted butter for brushing

Optional Glaze:
- 100 g icing sugar
- 2 tablespoons milk
- 1/2 teaspoon vanilla extract

ESTIMATED NUTRITIONAL INFORMATION PER DONUT:
Calories: approx. 180 kcal | Fat: approx. 6 g | Carbohydrates: approx. 25 g | Protein: approx. 3 g | Salt: approx. 0.2 g

INSTRUCTIONS:

1. **Prepare the dough:** In a mixing bowl, combine the flour, caster sugar, and yeast. Add the warm milk, melted butter, egg, and a pinch of salt. Mix until a dough forms, then knead for 5-7 minutes until smooth and elastic. Cover the dough and let it rise in a warm place for about 1 hour, or until doubled in size.

2. **Shape the donuts:** Once the dough has risen, roll it out on a lightly floured surface to about 1 cm thickness. Use a round cookie cutter to cut out donut shapes, and use a smaller cutter to cut out the centre holes. Re-roll the dough scraps to make more donuts.

3. **Air-fry the donuts:** Preheat the Ninja Air Fryer to the Air Crisp setting at 180°C (350°F). Lightly grease the air fryer basket and place the donuts inside, leaving space between them. Air-fry the donuts for 8-10 minutes, or until golden and cooked through, flipping halfway through.

4. **Coat or glaze the donuts:** Once the donuts are done, brush them with melted butter and toss in a mixture of sugar and cinnamon. Alternatively, whisk together the icing sugar, milk, and vanilla extract to make the glaze, and dip the donuts into the glaze while warm.

5. **Serve:** Serve the donuts warm, either coated in cinnamon sugar or with a sweet glaze. These air-fried donuts are a lighter version of the classic fried treat, but just as delicious.

RASPBERRY AND ALMOND TART

A sweet and tangy raspberry tart with a delicate almond filling, baked to perfection in the Ninja Air Fryer.

Portions: 6 | **Difficulty Level:** Medium | **Preparation Time:** 15 minutes | **Cooking Time:** 20-25 minutes | **Total Time:** 40 minutes

INGREDIENTS:

For the Pastry:
- 150 g plain flour
- 75 g unsalted butter, cold and cut into cubes
- 1 tablespoon caster sugar
- 1-2 tablespoons cold water

For the Filling:
- 100 g ground almonds
- 75 g unsalted butter, softened
- 75 g caster sugar
- 1 large egg
- 1 teaspoon vanilla extract
- 100 g fresh raspberries

ESTIMATED NUTRITIONAL INFORMATION PER SERVING:
Calories: approx. 320 kcal | Fat: approx. 20 g | Carbohydrates: approx. 30 g | Protein: approx. 5 g | Salt: approx. 0.2 g

INSTRUCTIONS:

1. **Make the pastry:** In a bowl, rub the cold butter into the flour until the mixture resembles breadcrumbs. Stir in the caster sugar, then gradually add the cold water until a dough forms. Wrap the dough in cling film and chill for 15 minutes.

2. **Prepare the filling:** In a separate bowl, cream together the softened butter and caster sugar until light and fluffy. Beat in the egg and vanilla extract, then fold in the ground almonds.

3. **Assemble the tart:** Preheat the Ninja Air Fryer to the Bake setting at 160°C (320°F). Roll out the pastry on a lightly floured surface and press it into an air fryer-safe tart tin. Spread the almond mixture evenly over the pastry base, then scatter the raspberries on top, gently pressing them into the filling.

4. **Bake the tart:** Place the tart in the air fryer basket and bake for 20-25 minutes, or until the filling is set and golden.

5. **Serve:** Allow the tart to cool slightly before slicing and serving. This tart is perfect as a sweet afternoon treat or dessert, with the tartness of the raspberries balancing the rich almond filling.

BREAD AND BUTTER PUDDING

A traditional British bread and butter pudding, air-baked with a creamy custard and a golden, crispy top.

Portions: 4 | **Difficulty Level:** Easy | **Preparation Time:** 10 minutes | **Cooking Time:** 15-18 minutes | **Total Time:** 25-28 minutes

INGREDIENTS:

- 4 slices of day-old bread (white or brioche), buttered
- 50 g raisins or sultanas (optional)
- 2 large eggs
- 300 ml whole milk
- 100 ml double cream
- 50 g caster sugar
- 1 teaspoon vanilla extract
- 1/2 teaspoon ground cinnamon (optional)
- Icing sugar for dusting (optional)

ESTIMATED NUTRITIONAL INFORMATION PER SERVING:
Calories: approx. 300 kcal | Fat: approx. 15 g | Carbohydrates: approx. 35 g | Protein: approx. 6 g | Salt: approx. 0.4 g

INSTRUCTIONS:

1. **Prepare the bread:** Butter the slices of bread on one side, then cut them into triangles or squares. Arrange the bread in an air fryer-safe dish, slightly overlapping the pieces. If using, scatter the raisins or sultanas between the layers of bread.
2. **Make the custard:** In a mixing bowl, whisk together the eggs, milk, double cream, caster sugar, vanilla extract, and cinnamon (if using) until well combined.
3. **Assemble the pudding:** Pour the custard mixture over the bread, making sure all the pieces are soaked. Let it sit for a few minutes to absorb.
4. **Bake the pudding:** Preheat the Ninja Air Fryer to the Bake setting at 160°C (320°F). Place the dish in the air fryer and bake for 15-18 minutes, or until the top is golden and the custard is set.
5. **Serve:** Allow the bread and butter pudding to cool slightly before serving. Dust with icing sugar if desired. This comforting dessert is perfect served warm with a scoop of ice cream or a drizzle of custard.

CHAPTER 6:
SAUCES, DIPS, AND CONDIMENTS

GARLIC AIOLI

A creamy garlic sauce perfect for dipping air-crisped vegetables or fries, made with fresh garlic and olive oil.

Portions: 4 | **Difficulty Level:** Easy | **Preparation Time:** 10 minutes | **Cooking Time**: 5 minutes (for roasting garlic) | **Total Time:** 15 minutes

INGREDIENTS:

- 2 large garlic cloves, peeled
- 1 egg yolk
- 1 teaspoon Dijon mustard
- 1 teaspoon lemon juice
- 150 ml olive oil
- Salt and freshly ground black pepper to taste

ESTIMATED NUTRITIONAL INFORMATION PER SERVING:
Calories: approx. 150 kcal | Fat: approx. 16 g | Carbohydrates: approx. 1 g | Protein: approx. 1 g | Salt: approx. 0.1 g

INSTRUCTIONS:

1. **Roast the garlic:** Preheat the Ninja Air Fryer to the Air Crisp setting at 180°C (350°F). Place the garlic cloves in the air fryer basket and roast for 5 minutes, or until soft and lightly browned.
2. **Make the aioli:** In a small bowl, mash the roasted garlic into a paste. Whisk in the egg yolk, Dijon mustard, and lemon juice until well combined.
3. **Add the olive oil:** Gradually drizzle in the olive oil while whisking continuously to create a thick and creamy sauce. Season with salt and freshly ground black pepper to taste.
4. **Serve:** Serve the garlic aioli as a dip for air-crisped vegetables, fries, or as a spread for sandwiches. This creamy sauce adds a delicious garlicky richness to any dish.

MINT YOGHOURT DIP

A refreshing yoghourt-based dip with mint, perfect for pairing with grilled meats, especially lamb dishes.

Portions: 4 | **Difficulty Level:** Easy | **Preparation Time:** 5 minutes | **Total Time:** 5 minutes

INGREDIENTS:

- 200 g Greek yoghourt
- 1 tablespoon fresh mint, finely chopped
- 1 tablespoon fresh coriander, finely chopped (optional)
- 1 tablespoon lemon juice
- 1 clove garlic, minced
- Salt and freshly ground black pepper to taste

ESTIMATED NUTRITIONAL INFORMATION PER SERVING:
Calories: approx. 50 kcal | Fat: approx. 2 g | Carbohydrates: approx. 3 g | Protein: approx. 5 g | Salt: approx. 0.2 g

INSTRUCTIONS:

1. **Mix the ingredients:** In a bowl, combine the Greek yoghourt, chopped mint, coriander (if using), lemon juice, and minced garlic. Stir until well mixed.
2. **Season to taste:** Add salt and freshly ground black pepper to taste, adjusting the seasoning as needed.
3. **Serve:** Serve the mint yoghourt dip chilled, as an accompaniment to grilled meats, kebabs, or as a refreshing dip for vegetables. This dip brings a cool and tangy flavour that complements rich and spicy dishes.

HOMEMADE TOMATO KETCHUP

A healthier, homemade version of ketchup, air-cooked for a rich tomato flavour, perfect for dipping or as a condiment.

Portions: 4 | **Difficulty Level:** Easy | **Preparation Time:** 5 minutes | **Cooking Time**: 20 minutes | **Total Time:** 25 minutes

INGREDIENTS:

- 400 g canned chopped tomatoes
- 1 small onion, finely chopped
- 1 clove garlic, minced
- 2 tablespoons brown sugar
- 2 tablespoons apple cider vinegar
- 1/2 teaspoon smoked paprika
- 1/4 teaspoon ground allspice
- Salt and freshly ground black pepper to taste

ESTIMATED NUTRITIONAL INFORMATION PER SERVING:
Calories: approx. 50 kcal | Fat: approx. 0.5 g | Carbohydrates: approx. 12 g | Protein: approx. 1 g | Salt: approx. 0.4 g

INSTRUCTIONS:

1. **Cook the onion and garlic:** Preheat the Ninja Air Fryer to the Bake setting at 160°C (320°F). In an air fryer-safe dish, combine the chopped onion and garlic. Air-bake for 5 minutes, until softened.
2. **Prepare the ketchup:** Add the chopped tomatoes, brown sugar, apple cider vinegar, smoked paprika, and allspice to the dish. Stir well to combine. Air-bake for another 15 minutes, stirring occasionally, until the mixture has thickened and reduced.
3. **Blend the ketchup:** Once the mixture has cooled slightly, transfer it to a blender or food processor and blend until smooth.
4. **Season and serve:** Adjust the seasoning with salt and freshly ground black pepper. Serve the homemade ketchup as a dip for fries, vegetables, or burgers. This ketchup has a rich, tangy flavour with a touch of sweetness.

HUMMUS WITH ROASTED GARLIC

Creamy homemade hummus with roasted garlic, air-roasted for extra flavour, perfect as a dip or spread.

Portions: 4 | **Difficulty Level:** Easy | **Preparation Time:** 10 minutes | **Cooking Time:** 5 minutes (for roasting garlic) | **Total Time:** 15 minutes

INGREDIENTS:

- 1 can (400 g) chickpeas, drained and rinsed
- 2 tablespoons tahini
- 2 large garlic cloves, peeled
- 2 tablespoons olive oil
- 1 tablespoon lemon juice
- 1 teaspoon ground cumin
- Salt and freshly ground black pepper to taste
- Water (as needed for consistency)

ESTIMATED NUTRITIONAL INFORMATION PER SERVING:
Calories: approx. 150 kcal | Fat: approx. 8 g | Carbohydrates: approx. 15 g | Protein: approx. 5 g | Salt: approx. 0.4 g

INSTRUCTIONS:

1. **Roast the garlic:** Preheat the Ninja Air Fryer to the Air Crisp setting at 180°C (350°F). Place the garlic cloves in the air fryer basket and roast for 5 minutes, or until softened and slightly browned.
2. **Make the hummus:** In a food processor, combine the roasted garlic, chickpeas, tahini, olive oil, lemon juice, cumin, salt, and pepper. Blend until smooth, adding water a tablespoon at a time until you reach your desired consistency.
3. **Serve:** Transfer the hummus to a serving bowl and drizzle with a little extra olive oil if desired. Serve with pita bread, crackers, or fresh vegetables for dipping.

BASIL PESTO

A fresh and vibrant basil pesto with olive oil and Parmesan, perfect for tossing with pasta or as a dip for bread and vegetables.

Portions: 4 | **Difficulty Level:** Easy | **Preparation Time:** 5 minutes | **Total Time:** 5 minutes

INGREDIENTS:

- 50 g fresh basil leaves
- 1 clove garlic, minced
- 30 g pine nuts
- 50 g grated Parmesan cheese
- 75 ml olive oil
- 1 tablespoon lemon juice
- Salt and freshly ground black pepper to taste

ESTIMATED NUTRITIONAL INFORMATION PER SERVING:
Calories: approx. 180 kcal | Fat: approx. 18 g | Carbohydrates: approx. 2 g | Protein: approx. 3 g | Salt: approx. 0.3 g

INSTRUCTIONS:

1. **Prepare the pesto:** In a food processor, combine the basil leaves, garlic, pine nuts, and grated Parmesan. Pulse until finely chopped. Gradually drizzle in the olive oil while continuing to blend until the mixture becomes a smooth paste.
2. **Add lemon juice and season:** Stir in the lemon juice and season with salt and freshly ground black pepper to taste.
3. **Serve:** Serve the basil pesto with pasta, spread on sandwiches, or as a dip for bread and vegetables. This fresh and vibrant pesto adds a delicious burst of flavour to any dish.

TZATZIKI WITH FRESH DILL

A tangy Greek yoghourt dip with cucumber and fresh dill, ideal for pairing with grilled meats or vegetables.

Portions: 4 | **Difficulty Level:** Easy | **Preparation Time:** 10 minutes | **Total Time:** 10 minutes

INGREDIENTS:

- 200 g Greek yoghourt
- 1/2 cucumber, grated
- 2 cloves garlic, minced
- 1 tablespoon fresh dill, finely chopped
- 1 tablespoon lemon juice
- 1 tablespoon olive oil
- Salt and freshly ground black pepper to taste

ESTIMATED NUTRITIONAL INFORMATION PER SERVING:
Calories: approx. 70 kcal | Fat: approx. 4 g | Carbohydrates: approx. 4 g | Protein: approx. 5 g | Salt: approx. 0.2 g

INSTRUCTIONS:

1. **Prepare the cucumber:** Grate the cucumber and squeeze out excess water using a clean kitchen towel or paper towel.
2. **Make the tzatziki:** In a bowl, combine the Greek yoghourt, grated cucumber, minced garlic, chopped dill, lemon juice, and olive oil. Stir until well combined.
3. **Season and serve:** Season with salt and freshly ground black pepper to taste. Serve chilled with grilled meats, pita bread, or as a dip for vegetables.

SWEET CHILLI SAUCE

A spicy and sweet chilli sauce, perfect for drizzling over crispy tofu, chicken, or as a dip for snacks.

Portions: 4 | **Difficulty Level:** Easy | **Preparation Time:** 5 minutes | **Cooking Time:** 10 minutes | **Total Time:** 15 minutes

INGREDIENTS:

- 100 g sugar
- 100 ml water
- 2 tablespoons rice vinegar
- 1 tablespoon soy sauce
- 2 cloves garlic, minced
- 1 red chilli, finely chopped
- 1 tablespoon cornflour mixed with 2 tablespoons water (for thickening)

ESTIMATED NUTRITIONAL INFORMATION PER SERVING:
Calories: approx. 70 kcal | Fat: approx. 0 g | Carbohydrates: approx. 17 g | Protein: approx. 1 g | Salt: approx. 0.3 g

INSTRUCTIONS:

1. **Prepare the sauce base:** In a small saucepan, combine the sugar, water, rice vinegar, soy sauce, minced garlic, and chopped chilli. Bring the mixture to a boil over medium heat, stirring until the sugar dissolves.
2. **Thicken the sauce:** Once the mixture boils, reduce the heat to low and simmer for 5 minutes. Stir in the cornflour slurry and cook for an additional 2-3 minutes, or until the sauce thickens.
3. **Cool and serve:** Remove the sauce from heat and let it cool. Serve as a dipping sauce for spring rolls, crispy tofu, chicken, or drizzle over grilled vegetables.

ROMESCO SAUCE

A rich and smoky sauce made with roasted red peppers, garlic, and almonds, perfect for serving with vegetables or seafood.

Portions: 4 | **Difficulty Level:** Easy | **Preparation Time:** 10 minutes | **Cooking Time**: 5 minutes | **Total Time:** 15 minutes

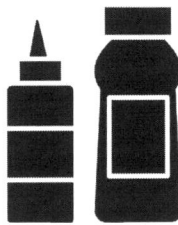

INGREDIENTS:

- 2 roasted red peppers (from a jar or roasted in the air fryer)
- 2 cloves garlic, peeled
- 30 g blanched almonds
- 1 slice of stale bread, torn into small pieces
- 2 tablespoons olive oil
- 1 tablespoon red wine vinegar
- 1/2 teaspoon smoked paprika
- Salt and freshly ground black pepper to taste

ESTIMATED NUTRITIONAL INFORMATION PER SERVING:
Calories: approx. 130 kcal | Fat: approx. 10 g | Carbohydrates: approx. 8 g | Protein: approx. 2 g | Salt: approx. 0.3 g

INSTRUCTIONS:

1. **Roast the garlic (if needed):** Preheat the Ninja Air Fryer to the Air Crisp setting at 180°C (350°F). Place the garlic cloves in the air fryer basket and roast for 5 minutes, until soft and lightly browned.
2. **Prepare the sauce:** In a food processor, combine the roasted red peppers, garlic, almonds, bread, olive oil, red wine vinegar, and smoked paprika. Blend until smooth, adding a little extra olive oil if needed for consistency.
3. **Season and serve:** Season the sauce with salt and freshly ground black pepper to taste. Serve with grilled vegetables, seafood, or as a dip for bread.

TAHINI DRESSING

A nutty and creamy tahini dressing, perfect for drizzling over salads or roasted vegetables.

Portions: 4 | **Difficulty Level:** Easy | **Preparation Time:** 5 minutes | **Total Time:** 5 minutes

INGREDIENTS:

- 3 tablespoons tahini
- 2 tablespoons lemon juice
- 1 tablespoon olive oil
- 1 clove garlic, minced
- 2 tablespoons water (more if needed)
- Salt and freshly ground black pepper to taste

ESTIMATED NUTRITIONAL INFORMATION PER SERVING:
Calories: approx. 100 kcal | Fat: approx. 9 g | Carbohydrates: approx. 3 g |
Protein: approx. 2 g | Salt: approx. 0.2 g

INSTRUCTIONS:

1. **Mix the ingredients:** In a small bowl, whisk together the tahini, lemon juice, olive oil, and minced garlic. Gradually add water, one tablespoon at a time, until the dressing reaches your desired consistency.
2. **Season and serve:** Season with salt and freshly ground black pepper to taste. Serve drizzled over salads, roasted vegetables, or as a dip for fresh vegetables.

BBQ SAUCE

A smoky homemade barbecue sauce, perfect for grilled meats, vegetables, or as a dipping sauce.

Portions: 4 | **Difficulty Level:** Easy | **Preparation Time:** 5 minutes |
Cooking Time: 10 minutes | **Total Time:** 15 minutes

INGREDIENTS:

- 100 g ketchup
- 2 tablespoons apple cider vinegar
- 2 tablespoons brown sugar
- 1 tablespoon Worcestershire sauce
- 1 tablespoon soy sauce
- 1 teaspoon smoked paprika
- 1 teaspoon mustard powder
- 1 clove garlic, minced
- 1/2 teaspoon ground black pepper

ESTIMATED NUTRITIONAL INFORMATION PER SERVING:
Calories: approx. 60 kcal | Fat: approx. 0.5 g | Carbohydrates: approx. 14 g |
Protein: approx. 1 g | Salt: approx. 0.6 g

INSTRUCTIONS:

1. **Mix the ingredients:** In a small saucepan, combine the ketchup, apple cider vinegar, brown sugar, Worcestershire sauce, soy sauce, smoked paprika, mustard powder, minced garlic, and black pepper.
2. **Cook the sauce:** Bring the mixture to a simmer over medium heat, stirring occasionally. Reduce the heat to low and cook for 10 minutes, or until the sauce thickens slightly.
3. **Cool and serve:** Remove the sauce from the heat and let it cool slightly before serving. Use as a glaze for grilled meats, a sauce for sandwiches, or as a dipping sauce for fries or vegetables.

CURRY SAUCE

A thick and flavourful curry sauce, perfect for serving with chips, naan bread, or over rice.

Portions: 4 | **Difficulty Level:** Easy | **Preparation Time:** 5 minutes |
Cooking Time: 15 minutes | **Total Time:** 20 minutes

INGREDIENTS:
- 1 small onion, finely chopped
- 2 cloves garlic, minced
- 1 tablespoon curry powder
- 1 teaspoon ground turmeric
- 1 teaspoon ground cumin
- 1 tablespoon tomato paste
- 250 ml vegetable or chicken stock
- 100 ml coconut milk
- 1 tablespoon flour (optional, for thickening)
- Salt and freshly ground black pepper to taste
- 1 tablespoon vegetable oil

ESTIMATED NUTRITIONAL INFORMATION PER SERVING:
Calories: approx. 100 kcal | Fat: approx. 5 g | Carbohydrates: approx. 12 g |
Protein: approx. 2 g | Salt: approx. 0.5 g

INSTRUCTIONS:
1. **Cook the onion and garlic:** In a saucepan, heat the vegetable oil over medium heat. Add the chopped onion and garlic, and sauté until softened, about 5 minutes.
2. **Add the spices:** Stir in the curry powder, turmeric, and cumin, and cook for 1 minute until fragrant.
3. **Add liquids and simmer:** Stir in the tomato paste, stock, and coconut milk. Bring the sauce to a simmer and cook for 10 minutes, stirring occasionally, until slightly thickened. If you prefer a thicker sauce, mix the flour with a little water to form a slurry and stir it into the sauce.
4. **Season and serve:** Season the curry sauce with salt and freshly ground black pepper to taste. Serve with chips, rice, or naan bread for a delicious, hearty side.

CHIMICHURRI

A vibrant green sauce with parsley, garlic, and olive oil, perfect for steak, grilled chicken, or vegetables.

Portions: 4 | **Difficulty Level:** Easy | **Preparation Time:** 5 minutes | **Total Time:** 5 minutes

INGREDIENTS:
- 50 g fresh parsley, finely chopped
- 2 cloves garlic, minced
- 1 teaspoon dried oregano
- 1/4 teaspoon red pepper flakes (optional)
- 2 tablespoons red wine vinegar
- 75 ml olive oil
- Salt and freshly ground black pepper to taste

ESTIMATED NUTRITIONAL INFORMATION PER SERVING:
Calories: approx. 130 kcal | Fat. approx. 14 g | Carbohydrates: approx. 1 g | Protein: approx. 1 g | Salt: approx. 0.2 g

INSTRUCTIONS:
1. **Mix the ingredients:** In a small bowl, combine the chopped parsley, minced garlic, dried oregano, and red pepper flakes (if using). Stir in the red wine vinegar and olive oil until well combined.
2. **Season and serve:** Season with salt and freshly ground black pepper to taste. Serve chimichurri as a sauce over steak, grilled chicken, or roasted vegetables for a burst of fresh, herby flavour.

HARISSA PASTE

A spicy North African paste made with chillies, garlic, and spices, perfect for adding heat and depth to grilled meats, vegetables, or sauces.

Portions: 4 | **Difficulty Level:** Medium | **Preparation Time:** 10 minutes | **Cooking Time**: 5 minutes (for roasting chillies) | **Total Time:** 15 minutes

INGREDIENTS:

- 4 dried red chillies, soaked in warm water for 10 minutes
- 1 teaspoon ground cumin
- 1 teaspoon ground coriander
- 1 teaspoon caraway seeds
- 3 cloves garlic, minced
- 2 tablespoons olive oil
- 1 tablespoon tomato paste
- 1 teaspoon smoked paprika
- 1 tablespoon lemon juice
- Salt and freshly ground black pepper to taste

ESTIMATED NUTRITIONAL INFORMATION PER SERVING:
Calories: approx. 70 kcal | Fat: approx. 6 g | Carbohydrates: approx. 5 g | Protein: approx. 1 g | Salt: approx. 0.4 g

INSTRUCTIONS:

1. **Roast the chillies:** Preheat the Ninja Air Fryer to the Air Crisp setting at 180°C (350°F). Place the soaked red chillies in the air fryer basket and roast for 5 minutes, until softened and lightly charred.
2. **Prepare the paste:** In a food processor, combine the roasted chillies, garlic, cumin, coriander, caraway seeds, olive oil, tomato paste, smoked paprika, and lemon juice. Blend until a smooth paste forms.
3. **Season and serve:** Season the harissa paste with salt and freshly ground black pepper to taste. Use harissa as a marinade for grilled meats, mix it into sauces, or serve as a spicy condiment.

LEMON AND HERB BUTTER

A zesty butter perfect for spreading over grilled fish, chicken, or vegetables, adding fresh lemony flavour with a hint of herbs.

Portions: 4 | **Difficulty Level:** Easy | **Preparation Time:** 5 minutes | **Total Time:** 5 minutes

INGREDIENTS:

- 100 g unsalted butter, softened
- Zest of 1 lemon
- 1 tablespoon lemon juice
- 1 tablespoon fresh parsley, finely chopped
- 1 teaspoon fresh thyme, finely chopped
- Salt and freshly ground black pepper to taste

ESTIMATED NUTRITIONAL INFORMATION PER SERVING:
Calories: approx. 130 kcal | Fat: approx. 14 g | Carbohydrates: approx. 0.5 g | Protein: approx. 0.5 g | Salt: approx. 0.1 g

INSTRUCTIONS:

1. **Prepare the butter:** In a small bowl, mix together the softened butter, lemon zest, lemon juice, parsley, and thyme until well combined.
2. **Season and serve:** Season the butter with salt and freshly ground black pepper to taste. Use the lemon and herb butter to spread over grilled fish, chicken, or vegetables for a burst of fresh flavour.

SALSA VERDE

A fresh and tangy green sauce made with herbs, capers, and olive oil, perfect for drizzling over grilled vegetables, fish, or meats.

Portions: 4 | **Difficulty Level:** Easy | **Preparation Time:** 5 minutes | **Total Time:** 5 minutes

INGREDIENTS:

- 50 g fresh parsley, finely chopped
- 1 tablespoon capers, rinsed and drained
- 2 anchovy fillets (optional), finely chopped
- 1 clove garlic, minced
- 2 tablespoons red wine vinegar
- 75 ml olive oil
- Salt and freshly ground black pepper to taste

ESTIMATED NUTRITIONAL INFORMATION PER SERVING:
Calories: approx. 120 kcal | Fat: approx. 12 g | Carbohydrates: approx. 1 g | Protein: approx. 1 g | Salt: approx. 0.4 g

INSTRUCTIONS:

1. **Mix the ingredients:** In a small bowl, combine the chopped parsley, capers, anchovy fillets (if using), and minced garlic. Stir in the red wine vinegar and olive oil until well combined.
2. **Season and serve:** Season with salt and freshly ground black pepper to taste. Drizzle the salsa verde over grilled vegetables, fish, or meats for a bright and herby finish.

CHAPTER 7:
VEGETARIAN & VEGAN DISHES

CRISPY TOFU WITH SESAME AND SOY

Air-fried tofu cubes coated in a sesame-soy glaze, perfect for serving with rice or salad.

Portions: 4 | **Difficulty Level:** Easy | **Preparation Time:** 10 minutes |
Cooking Time: 15 minutes | **Total Time:** 25 minutes

INGREDIENTS:

- 400 g firm tofu, drained and cubed
- 2 tablespoons soy sauce
- 1 tablespoon sesame oil
- 1 tablespoon cornstarch
- 1 teaspoon rice vinegar
- 1 tablespoon sesame seeds
- 2 spring onions, finely chopped (for garnish)
- Salt and freshly ground black pepper to taste

ESTIMATED NUTRITIONAL INFORMATION PER SERVING:
Calories: approx. 180 kcal | Fat: approx. 12 g | Carbohydrates: approx. 6 g |
Protein: approx. 12 g | Salt: approx. 1.0 g

INSTRUCTIONS:

1. **Prepare the tofu:** Preheat the Ninja Air Fryer to the Air Crisp setting at 180°C (350°F). Pat the tofu dry and toss the cubes with cornstarch to coat evenly.
2. **Air-fry the tofu:** Place the tofu cubes in the air fryer basket in a single layer. Air-fry for 12-15 minutes, shaking the basket halfway through, until golden and crispy.
3. **Make the glaze:** While the tofu is cooking, whisk together the soy sauce, sesame oil, and rice vinegar in a bowl.
4. **Coat the tofu:** Once the tofu is crispy, transfer it to a bowl and toss it with the sesame-soy glaze. Sprinkle with sesame seeds and garnish with chopped spring onions.
5. **Serve:** Serve the crispy tofu over rice or salad. This dish is delicious with a side of steamed vegetables or stir-fried greens.

STUFFED AUBERGINES WITH LENTILS AND TOMATOES

Aubergine halves stuffed with a rich lentil and tomato filling, air-roasted for a tender finish.

Portions: 4 | **Difficulty Level:** Medium | **Preparation Time:** 15 minutes |
Cooking Time: 20 minutes | **Total Time:** 35 minutes

INGREDIENTS:

- 2 large aubergines, halved and flesh scooped out
- 200 g cooked green or brown lentils
- 1 onion, finely chopped
- 2 cloves garlic, minced
- 1 can (400 g) chopped tomatoes
- 1 tablespoon olive oil
- 1 teaspoon ground cumin
- 1 teaspoon smoked paprika
- 1 tablespoon fresh parsley, chopped (for garnish)
- Salt and freshly ground black pepper to taste

ESTIMATED NUTRITIONAL INFORMATION PER SERVING:
Calories: approx. 220 kcal | Fat: approx. 8 g | Carbohydrates: approx. 30 g |
Protein: approx. 8 g | Salt: approx. 0.6 g

INSTRUCTIONS:

1. **Prepare the aubergines:** Preheat the Ninja Air Fryer to the Air Crisp setting at 180°C (350°F). Brush the aubergine halves with olive oil and season with salt and pepper. Air-fry the aubergine halves for 10-12 minutes, until softened.
2. **Make the filling:** In a pan, heat a tablespoon of olive oil over medium heat. Add the chopped onion and garlic and sauté until softened, about 5 minutes. Stir in the cumin, smoked paprika, lentils, and chopped tomatoes. Simmer for 10 minutes until thickened. Season with salt and pepper.
3. **Stuff the aubergines:** Remove the softened aubergines from the air fryer and fill each half with the lentil and tomato mixture.
4. **Air-fry the stuffed aubergines:** Return the stuffed aubergines to the air fryer and cook for an additional 8 minutes at 180°C (350°F), until the filling is heated through and the aubergines are tender.
5. **Serve:** Garnish the stuffed aubergines with fresh parsley and serve warm. This hearty dish pairs well with a side salad or roasted vegetables.

CAULIFLOWER STEAKS WITH HARISSA SAUCE

Thick cauliflower steaks brushed with spicy harissa sauce, air-roasted to perfection.

Portions: 4 | **Difficulty Level:** Easy | **Preparation Time:** 10 minutes | **Cooking Time:** 15-18 minutes | **Total Time:** 25-28 minutes

INGREDIENTS:

- 1 large cauliflower, cut into 4 thick steaks
- 2 tablespoons olive oil
- 2 tablespoons harissa paste
- 1 tablespoon lemon juice
- Salt and freshly ground black pepper to taste
- Fresh parsley, chopped (for garnish)

ESTIMATED NUTRITIONAL INFORMATION PER SERVING:
Calories: approx. 120 kcal | Fat: approx. 8 g | Carbohydrates: approx. 10 g | Protein: approx. 3 g | Salt: approx. 0.5 g

INSTRUCTIONS:

1. **Prepare the cauliflower steaks:** Preheat the Ninja Air Fryer to the Air Crisp setting at 180°C (350°F). Brush both sides of the cauliflower steaks with olive oil and season with salt and freshly ground black pepper.
2. **Air-fry the cauliflower steaks:** Place the cauliflower steaks in the air fryer basket in a single layer. Air-fry for 15-18 minutes, flipping halfway through, until golden and tender.
3. **Make the harissa sauce:** In a small bowl, mix the harissa paste with lemon juice.
4. **Coat the steaks:** Once the cauliflower steaks are done, brush them with the harissa sauce while still hot.
5. **Serve:** Garnish with chopped fresh parsley and serve with a side of couscous or salad. These cauliflower steaks are packed with bold flavours and make a great vegetarian main or side dish.

VEGAN MEATBALLS IN TOMATO SAUCE

Plant-based meatballs air-fried and served in a rich tomato sauce, perfect for a hearty, comforting meal.

Portions: 4 | **Difficulty Level:** Medium | **Preparation Time:** 15 minutes | **Cooking Time:** 20 minutes | **Total Time:** 35 minutes

INGREDIENTS:

For the Meatballs:
- 200 g cooked lentils
- 100 g breadcrumbs
- 1 tablespoon flaxseed meal mixed with 3 tablespoons water (for a flax egg)
- 1 onion, finely chopped
- 2 cloves garlic, minced
- 1 tablespoon olive oil
- 1 teaspoon dried oregano
- 1 teaspoon smoked paprika
- Salt and freshly ground black pepper to taste

For the Tomato Sauce:
- 1 can (400 g) chopped tomatoes
- 1 tablespoon olive oil
- 1 small onion, finely chopped
- 2 cloves garlic, minced
- 1 teaspoon dried basil
- 1 teaspoon dried oregano
- Salt and freshly ground black pepper to taste

ESTIMATED NUTRITIONAL INFORMATION PER SERVING:
Calories: approx. 250 kcal | Fat: approx. 10 g | Carbohydrates: approx. 30 g | Protein: approx. 10 g | Salt: approx. 0.7 g

INSTRUCTIONS:

1. **Make the vegan meatballs:** Preheat the Ninja Air Fryer to the Air Crisp setting at 180°C (350°F). In a frying pan, heat olive oil over medium heat and sauté the onion and garlic until soft. In a large bowl, combine the lentils, breadcrumbs, flax egg, sautéed onion and garlic, oregano, smoked paprika, salt, and pepper. Mix well and form the mixture into small meatballs.

2. **Air-fry the meatballs:** Place the meatballs in the air fryer basket in a single layer and air-fry for 10-12 minutes, shaking the basket halfway through, until the meatballs are crispy on the outside.

3. **Prepare the tomato sauce:** In a saucepan, heat olive oil over medium heat. Add the onion and garlic and sauté until soft. Stir in the chopped tomatoes, basil, oregano, salt, and pepper. Simmer the sauce for 10-15 minutes until it thickens.

4. **Serve:** Serve the vegan meatballs hot, topped with the tomato sauce. These plant-based meatballs are perfect with pasta, rice, or a side of crusty bread.

GRILLED VEGETABLE SKEWERS WITH TAHINI

Colourful vegetable skewers grilled and served with a creamy tahini dip, perfect for a light meal or side dish.

Portions: 4 | **Difficulty Level:** Easy | **Preparation Time:** 10 minutes | **Cooking Time:** 10 minutes | **Total Time:** 20 minutes

INGREDIENTS:

For the Skewers:
- 1 red bell pepper, cut into chunks
- 1 yellow bell pepper, cut into chunks
- 1 courgette, sliced
- 1 red onion, cut into wedges
- 8 cherry tomatoes
- 1 tablespoon olive oil
- Salt and freshly ground black pepper to taste

- Wooden or metal skewers

For the Tahini Dip:
- 3 tablespoons tahini
- 2 tablespoons lemon juice
- 1 clove garlic, minced
- 2 tablespoons water (or more if needed)
- Salt and freshly ground black pepper to taste

ESTIMATED NUTRITIONAL INFORMATION PER SERVING:
Calories: approx. 180 kcal | Fat: approx. 12 g | Carbohydrates: approx. 14 g | Protein: approx. 4 g | Salt: approx. 0.5 g

INSTRUCTIONS:

1. **Prepare the vegetables:** Preheat the Ninja Air Fryer to the Air Crisp setting at 180°C (350°F). Toss the bell peppers, courgette, red onion, and cherry tomatoes in olive oil. Season with salt and freshly ground black pepper.
2. **Assemble the skewers:** Thread the vegetables onto the skewers, alternating between the different types.
3. **Air-fry the skewers:** Place the skewers in the air fryer basket in a single layer and cook for 10 minutes, turning halfway through, until the vegetables are tender and lightly charred.
4. **Make the tahini dip:** In a small bowl, whisk together the tahini, lemon juice, minced garlic, and water until smooth. Add more water if needed to achieve the desired consistency. Season with salt and pepper.
5. **Serve:** Serve the grilled vegetable skewers with the tahini dip on the side. These vibrant and delicious skewers are perfect as a main or side dish.

MUSHROOM AND SPINACH WELLINGTON

A flaky mushroom and spinach Wellington, air-baked to golden perfection, perfect for a special occasion or dinner party.

Portions: 4 | **Difficulty Level:** Medium | **Preparation Time:** 15 minutes | **Cooking Time:** 20 minutes | **Total Time:** 35 minutes

INGREDIENTS:

- 1 sheet of puff pastry (ready-made, vegan if needed)
- 250 g mushrooms, finely chopped
- 100 g fresh spinach
- 1 onion, finely chopped
- 2 cloves garlic, minced
- 1 tablespoon olive oil
- 1 teaspoon fresh thyme leaves
- 1 tablespoon Dijon mustard
- 1 tablespoon soy sauce
- Salt and freshly ground black pepper to taste
- 1 tablespoon plant-based milk (for brushing)

ESTIMATED NUTRITIONAL INFORMATION PER SERVING:
Calories: approx. 300 kcal | Fat: approx. 18 g | Carbohydrates: approx. 25 g | Protein: approx. 6 g | Salt: approx. 0.8 g

INSTRUCTIONS:

1. **Prepare the filling:** Preheat the Ninja Air Fryer to the Bake setting at 180°C (350°F). In a frying pan, heat olive oil over medium heat. Sauté the onion and garlic until softened. Add the mushrooms and cook until they release their moisture, about 5 minutes. Stir in the spinach, thyme, Dijon mustard, and soy sauce. Cook until the spinach wilts and the mixture is thickened. Season with salt and pepper.
2. **Assemble the Wellington:** Roll out the puff pastry and place the mushroom and spinach mixture in the centre. Fold the pastry over the filling, sealing the edges to form a neat parcel. Brush the top with plant-based milk.
3. **Bake the Wellington:** Place the Wellington in the air fryer basket and bake for 15-20 minutes, or until the pastry is golden and crisp.
4. **Serve:** Slice the Wellington and serve hot. This elegant dish pairs beautifully with a side salad or roasted vegetables.

CHICKPEA AND SPINACH CURRY

A hearty chickpea curry made with fresh spinach and a blend of spices, cooked using the Roast function in the Ninja Air Fryer.

Portions: 4 | **Difficulty Level:** Easy | **Preparation Time:** 10 minutes | **Cooking Time**: 20 minutes | **Total Time:** 30 minutes

INGREDIENTS:

- 1 can (400 g) chickpeas, drained and rinsed
- 100 g fresh spinach
- 1 onion, finely chopped
- 2 cloves garlic, minced
- 1 tablespoon fresh ginger, grated
- 1 can (400 g) chopped tomatoes
- 1 tablespoon olive oil
- 1 teaspoon ground cumin
- 1 teaspoon ground coriander
- 1 teaspoon turmeric
- 1 teaspoon garam masala
- Salt and freshly ground black pepper to taste
- Fresh coriander leaves (for garnish)

ESTIMATED NUTRITIONAL INFORMATION PER SERVING:
Calories: approx. 200 kcal | Fat: approx. 8 g | Carbohydrates: approx. 25 g | Protein: approx. 6 g | Salt: approx. 0.7 g

INSTRUCTIONS:

1. **Prepare the curry base:** Preheat the Ninja Air Fryer to the Roast setting at 180°C (350°F). In a frying pan, heat olive oil over medium heat. Add the chopped onion, garlic, and ginger, and sauté until softened.
2. **Add the spices and chickpeas:** Stir in the ground cumin, coriander, turmeric, and garam masala. Add the chickpeas and chopped tomatoes, and simmer for 10 minutes until the sauce thickens slightly.
3. **Add the spinach:** Stir in the fresh spinach and cook for an additional 5 minutes until wilted.
4. **Serve:** Serve the chickpea and spinach curry hot, garnished with fresh coriander. Pair with rice or naan for a complete meal.

STUFFED BELL PEPPERS WITH COUSCOUS

Bell peppers stuffed with a savoury couscous and vegetable mixture, air-baked until tender.

Portions: 4 | **Difficulty Level:** Easy | **Preparation Time:** 10 minutes |
Cooking Time: 15 minutes | **Total Time:** 25 minutes

INGREDIENTS:

- 4 large bell peppers, tops cut off and seeds removed
- 200 g couscous
- 1 small onion, finely chopped
- 1 zucchini, diced
- 1 tomato, chopped
- 1 tablespoon olive oil
- 1 teaspoon ground cumin
- 1 teaspoon paprika
- 1 tablespoon fresh parsley, chopped
- Salt and freshly ground black pepper to taste

ESTIMATED NUTRITIONAL INFORMATION PER SERVING:
Calories: approx. 220 kcal | Fat: approx. 8 g | Carbohydrates: approx. 35 g |
Protein: approx. 5 g | Salt: approx. 0.6 g

INSTRUCTIONS:

1. **Prepare the couscous:** Cook the couscous according to package instructions. Fluff with a fork and set aside.
2. **Cook the vegetables:** In a frying pan, heat olive oil over medium heat. Add the onion, zucchini, and tomato, and sauté until softened, about 5 minutes. Stir in the cumin and paprika, and season with salt and pepper. Mix in the couscous and fresh parsley.
3. **Stuff the bell peppers:** Preheat the Ninja Air Fryer to the Air Crisp setting at 180°C (350°F). Stuff each bell pepper with the couscous and vegetable mixture.
4. **Air-fry the peppers:** Place the stuffed peppers in the air fryer basket and cook for 10-15 minutes, until the peppers are tender and slightly charred on the edges.
5. **Serve:** Serve the stuffed peppers hot. This light yet hearty dish is perfect as a main course or side.

VEGAN SHEPHERD'S PIE

A plant-based version of the classic shepherd's pie, made with a rich lentil filling and air-baked mashed potato topping.

Portions: 4 | **Difficulty Level:** Medium | **Preparation Time:** 15 minutes |
Cooking Time: 25 minutes | **Total Time:** 40 minutes

INGREDIENTS:

For the Filling:
- 1 can (400 g) lentils, drained and rinsed
- 1 onion, finely chopped
- 2 carrots, diced
- 1 celery stalk, diced
- 2 cloves garlic, minced
- 1 tablespoon olive oil
- 1 tablespoon tomato paste
- 200 ml vegetable stock
- 1 teaspoon dried thyme
- Salt and freshly ground black pepper to taste

For the Mashed Potato Topping:
- 4 large potatoes, peeled and chopped
- 2 tablespoons plant-based butter
- 100 ml plant-based milk
- Salt and freshly ground black pepper to taste

ESTIMATED NUTRITIONAL INFORMATION PER SERVING:
Calories: approx. 300 kcal | Fat: approx. 10 g | Carbohydrates: approx. 45 g |
Protein: approx. 8 g | Salt: approx. 0.7 g

INSTRUCTIONS:

1. **Prepare the filling:** Preheat the Ninja Air Fryer to the Air Crisp setting at 180°C (350°F). In a frying pan, heat olive oil over medium heat. Sauté the onion, carrots, celery, and garlic until softened. Stir in the lentils, tomato paste, vegetable stock, and thyme. Simmer for 10 minutes until thickened. Season with salt and pepper.
2. **Make the mashed potato topping:** While the filling is cooking, boil the potatoes in salted water until tender. Drain and mash with plant-based butter and milk until smooth. Season with salt and pepper.
3. **Assemble the shepherd's pie:** Spoon the lentil filling into an air fryer-safe baking dish. Spread the mashed potatoes evenly on top.
4. **Air-bake the shepherd's pie:** Place the dish in the air fryer and cook for 15 minutes, or until the top is golden and crispy.
5. **Serve:** Serve hot and enjoy. This hearty, comforting dish is perfect for a family meal.

CRISPY FALAFEL WRAPS

Golden, crispy falafel served in a wrap with fresh veggies and tahini sauce, perfect for a light and satisfying meal.

Portions: 4 | **Difficulty Level:** Easy | **Preparation Time:** 10 minutes | **Cooking Time**: 15 minutes | **Total Time:** 25 minutes

INGREDIENTS:

For the Falafel:
- 1 can (400 g) chickpeas, drained and rinsed
- 1 small onion, finely chopped
- 2 cloves garlic, minced
- 2 tablespoons fresh parsley, chopped
- 1 teaspoon ground cumin
- 1 teaspoon ground coriander
- 2 tablespoons flour (or chickpea flour for gluten-free)
- Salt and freshly ground black pepper to taste

For the Wraps:
- 4 large wraps or flatbreads
- Fresh lettuce, chopped
- 1 tomato, sliced
- 1 cucumber, sliced
- 4 tablespoons tahini sauce

ESTIMATED NUTRITIONAL INFORMATION PER SERVING:
Calories: approx. 300 kcal | Fat: approx. 10 g | Carbohydrates: approx. 40 g | Protein: approx. 10 g | Salt: approx. 0.8 g

INSTRUCTIONS:

1. **Prepare the falafel mixture:** In a food processor, combine the chickpeas, onion, garlic, parsley, cumin, coriander, flour, salt, and pepper. Pulse until the mixture comes together but still has some texture.
2. **Shape the falafel:** Form the mixture into small falafel balls or patties.
3. **Air-fry the falafel:** Preheat the Ninja Air Fryer to the Air Crisp setting at 180°C (350°F). Place the falafel in the air fryer basket in a single layer and cook for 12-15 minutes, shaking the basket halfway through, until golden and crispy.
4. **Assemble the wraps:** Spread a tablespoon of tahini sauce onto each wrap or flatbread. Add lettuce, tomato, and cucumber, then top with the crispy falafel.
5. **Serve:** Roll up the wraps and serve immediately. These falafel wraps are perfect for a quick, healthy meal or snack.

GRILLED VEGGIE BURGERS

Plant-based burgers grilled until golden and served with your favourite toppings, a perfect vegetarian option for a satisfying meal.

Portions: 4 | **Difficulty Level:** Easy | **Preparation Time:** 10 minutes | **Cooking Time**: 12 minutes | **Total Time:** 22 minutes

INGREDIENTS:

- 1 can (400 g) black beans, drained and rinsed
- 1 small onion, finely chopped
- 2 cloves garlic, minced
- 1 small carrot, grated
- 50 g breadcrumbs
- 1 teaspoon ground cumin
- 1 teaspoon paprika

- 1 tablespoon soy sauce
- 1 tablespoon olive oil
- Salt and freshly ground black pepper to taste
- 4 burger buns
- Toppings: lettuce, tomato, onion, avocado, ketchup, mustard (optional)

ESTIMATED NUTRITIONAL INFORMATION PER SERVING:
Calories: approx. 300 kcal | Fat: approx. 8 g | Carbohydrates: approx. 45 g | Protein: approx. 10 g | Salt: approx. 0.9 g

INSTRUCTIONS:

1. **Prepare the veggie burger mixture:** In a large bowl, mash the black beans with a fork until mostly smooth. Stir in the chopped onion, garlic, grated carrot, breadcrumbs, cumin, paprika, soy sauce, and olive oil. Season with salt and pepper.
2. **Shape the patties:** Form the mixture into 4 equal-sized patties.
3. **Air-fry the veggie burgers:** Preheat the Ninja Air Fryer to the Grill setting at 180°C (350°F). Place the patties in the air fryer basket and cook for 10-12 minutes, flipping halfway through, until golden and firm.
4. **Assemble the burgers:** Toast the burger buns and add your favourite toppings, such as lettuce, tomato, onion, and avocado. Place the veggie burgers on the buns and top with ketchup, mustard, or other condiments of choice.
5. **Serve:** Serve the veggie burgers hot with a side of fries or a salad. These flavourful veggie burgers are a great meat-free alternative that everyone will love.

STUFFED MUSHROOMS WITH GARLIC AND HERBS

Large mushrooms stuffed with garlic, herbs, and breadcrumbs, air-roasted until crispy and golden.

Portions: 4 | **Difficulty Level:** Easy | **Preparation Time:** 10 minutes | **Cooking Time:** 10 minutes | **Total Time:** 20 minutes

INGREDIENTS:

- 8 large mushrooms, stems removed
- 2 tablespoons olive oil
- 3 cloves garlic, minced
- 3 tablespoons breadcrumbs
- 2 tablespoons fresh parsley, chopped
- 1 teaspoon fresh thyme leaves
- Salt and freshly ground black pepper to taste
- 1 tablespoon grated vegan Parmesan (optional)

ESTIMATED NUTRITIONAL INFORMATION PER SERVING:
Calories: approx. 120 kcal | Fat: approx. 8 g | Carbohydrates: approx. 10 g | Protein: approx. 3 g | Salt: approx. 0.4 g

INSTRUCTIONS:

1. **Prepare the mushrooms:** Preheat the Ninja Air Fryer to the Air Crisp setting at 180°C (350°F). In a bowl, toss the mushroom caps with olive oil, salt, and pepper. Set aside.
2. **Make the filling:** In a small bowl, mix together the garlic, breadcrumbs, parsley, thyme, and grated vegan Parmesan (if using). Season with salt and pepper.
3. **Stuff the mushrooms:** Spoon the garlic and herb mixture into each mushroom cap, pressing down lightly.
4. **Air-fry the stuffed mushrooms:** Place the stuffed mushrooms in the air fryer basket in a single layer and cook for 8-10 minutes, until the mushrooms are tender and the tops are golden and crispy.
5. **Serve:** Serve the stuffed mushrooms hot as an appetiser or side dish. These savoury bites are perfect for parties or as a simple starter.

AIR-FRIED ZUCCHINI FRITTERS

Crispy zucchini fritters served with a lemon yoghourt dip, perfect for a light snack or appetiser.

Portions: 4 | **Difficulty Level:** Easy | **Preparation Time:** 10 minutes |
Cooking Time: 12 minutes | **Total Time:** 22 minutes

INGREDIENTS:

- 2 medium zucchinis, grated
- 1 small onion, finely chopped
- 1 clove garlic, minced
- 1 egg (or flax egg for vegan option)
- 50 g breadcrumbs
- 1 tablespoon fresh parsley, chopped
- 1 teaspoon ground cumin
- Salt and freshly ground black pepper to taste

- Olive oil spray (for air-frying)

For the Lemon Yoghourt Dip:
- 100 g Greek yoghourt (or plant-based yoghourt)
- 1 tablespoon lemon juice
- 1 tablespoon fresh dill, chopped
- Salt and freshly ground black pepper to taste

ESTIMATED NUTRITIONAL INFORMATION PER SERVING:
Calories: approx. 180 kcal | Fat: approx. 10 g | Carbohydrates: approx. 15 g |
Protein: approx. 6 g | Salt: approx. 0.5 g

INSTRUCTIONS:

1. **Prepare the fritter mixture:** In a large bowl, mix the grated zucchini with a pinch of salt and let it sit for 5 minutes. Squeeze out any excess moisture from the zucchini, then combine it with the chopped onion, garlic, egg, breadcrumbs, parsley, cumin, salt, and pepper. Stir until well combined.
2. **Shape the fritters:** Form the mixture into small patties.
3. **Air-fry the fritters:** Preheat the Ninja Air Fryer to the Air Crisp setting at 180°C (350°F). Lightly spray the fritters with olive oil and place them in the air fryer basket in a single layer. Air-fry for 10-12 minutes, flipping halfway through, until golden and crispy.
4. **Make the lemon yoghourt dip:** In a small bowl, whisk together the Greek yoghourt, lemon juice, dill, salt, and pepper.
5. **Serve:** Serve the crispy zucchini fritters hot with the lemon yoghourt dip on the side. These fritters are perfect for dipping and make a great snack or starter.

SWEET POTATO AND CHICKPEA TAGINE

A Moroccan-inspired tagine made with sweet potato and chickpeas, slow-roasted for depth of flavour.

Portions: 4 | **Difficulty Level:** Medium | **Preparation Time:** 15 minutes | **Cooking Time**: 20 minutes | **Total Time:** 35 minutes

INGREDIENTS:

- 2 medium sweet potatoes, peeled and cubed
- 1 can (400 g) chickpeas, drained and rinsed
- 1 onion, finely chopped
- 2 cloves garlic, minced
- 1 tablespoon olive oil
- 1 teaspoon ground cumin
- 1 teaspoon ground cinnamon
- 1 teaspoon ground coriander
- 1 teaspoon ground turmeric
- 400 ml vegetable stock
- 1 can (400 g) chopped tomatoes
- 1 tablespoon fresh parsley or coriander, chopped (for garnish)
- Salt and freshly ground black pepper to taste

ESTIMATED NUTRITIONAL INFORMATION PER SERVING:
Calories: approx. 280 kcal | Fat: approx. 8 g | Carbohydrates: approx. 45 g | Protein: approx. 7 g | Salt: approx. 0.6 g

INSTRUCTIONS:

1. **Prepare the tagine base:** Preheat the Ninja Air Fryer to the Roast setting at 180°C (350°F). In a large pan, heat the olive oil over medium heat. Sauté the chopped onion and garlic until softened, about 5 minutes. Stir in the cumin, cinnamon, coriander, and turmeric, and cook for another minute until fragrant.
2. **Add the vegetables:** Stir in the cubed sweet potatoes, chickpeas, chopped tomatoes, and vegetable stock. Season with salt and pepper. Simmer for 5 minutes.
3. **Air-roast the tagine:** Transfer the mixture to an air fryer-safe baking dish and roast in the air fryer for 15-20 minutes, or until the sweet potatoes are tender and the flavours are well combined.
4. **Serve:** Garnish the tagine with fresh parsley or coriander and serve hot with couscous or flatbread. This hearty, spiced dish is perfect for a comforting meal.

ROASTED RED PEPPER AND TOMATO SOUP

A smoky, rich roasted red pepper soup made in the Ninja Air Fryer, perfect for a light and comforting meal.

Portions: 4 | **Difficulty Level:** Easy | **Preparation Time:** 10 minutes | **Cooking Time:** 20 minutes | **Total Time:** 30 minutes

INGREDIENTS:

- 3 large red bell peppers, halved and seeds removed
- 4 large tomatoes, halved
- 1 onion, quartered
- 3 cloves garlic, peeled
- 1 tablespoon olive oil
- 500 ml vegetable stock
- 1 teaspoon smoked paprika
- Salt and freshly ground black pepper to taste
- Fresh basil leaves (for garnish)

ESTIMATED NUTRITIONAL INFORMATION PER SERVING:
Calories: approx. 120 kcal | Fat: approx. 6 g | Carbohydrates: approx. 18 g | Protein: approx. 3 g | Salt: approx. 0.5 g

INSTRUCTIONS:

1. **Roast the vegetables:** Preheat the Ninja Air Fryer to the Roast setting at 180°C (350°F). Toss the red bell peppers, tomatoes, onion, and garlic in olive oil and season with salt and pepper. Place the vegetables in the air fryer basket and roast for 15-20 minutes, or until the vegetables are soft and slightly charred.
2. **Blend the soup:** Once the vegetables are roasted, transfer them to a blender. Add the smoked paprika and vegetable stock, and blend until smooth. Adjust seasoning with salt and pepper if needed.
3. **Heat and serve:** Pour the soup into a pot and heat over medium heat until warmed through. Garnish with fresh basil leaves and serve hot with crusty bread. This rich and smoky soup is perfect for a light lunch or dinner.

DISCLAIMER

This cookbook, „Ninja Air Fryer Cookbook UK: The XXL Air Fryer Recipe Book with Quick, Delicious & Mouthwatering Dishes for Daily Enjoyment," is intended for informational and educational purposes only. The recipes and nutritional information provided in this book are based on general guidelines and may not suit individual dietary requirements or preferences. It is recommended that readers consult a qualified health professional or nutritionist to ensure that the recipes align with their specific health conditions or dietary needs.

The nutritional information included in this cookbook is an approximation and may vary depending on ingredient brands, portion sizes, and cooking methods. The publisher, author, and any affiliated parties are not responsible for any adverse effects, allergies, or issues that may arise from following the recipes in this book.

This book is not endorsed by or affiliated with Ninja or any related brands. All trademarks and product names are the property of their respective owners.

EXCLUSIVE BONUS

40 Weight Loss Recipes

&

14 Days Meal Plan

Scan the QR-Code and receive
the FREE download:

Printed in Great Britain
by Amazon

51528786R00081